12/08   24.95

DO
CATS
HEAR
WITH THEIR
FEET?

ILLUSTRATIONS BY JAKE PAGE

PHOTOGRAPHS BY SUSANNE PAGE
(except as noted)

PREFACE BY MICHAEL W. FOX

Smithsonian Books

Collins
An Imprint of HarperCollinsPublishers

DO CATS HEAR WITH THEIR FEET?

Where Cats
Come From, What We Know
About Them, and
What They Think About Us

JAKE PAGE

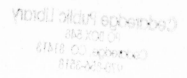

Photographs for Introduction and Chapters One through Nine © Susanne Page; Chapter Ten © Kendall Barrett; Chapter Eleven © Sally Stone Halvorson. All illustrations appearing within the text © Jake Page.

HarperCollins books may be purchased for educational, business, or sales promotional use. For information, please write: Special Markets Department, HarperCollins Publishers, 10 East 53rd Street, New York, NY 10022.

FIRST EDITION

Designed by Chris Welch

Library of Congress Cataloging-in-Publication Data is available upon request.
ISBN 978-0-06-145648-0

08 09 10 11 12 OV/RRD 10 9 8 7 6 5 4 3 2 1

FOR SUSANNE, AS ALWAYS,
NOT TO MENTION
CAT, RUDOLPH, AND FIG NEWTON

CONTENTS

PART THREE
THE CAT'S WORLD

APPENDICES

PREFACE

As a veterinarian and animal behaviorist, I tend to approach animals and the books about them I review the same way. Like taking a cat's temperature, I first check the back end as soon as I have glanced at the cover.

I look for reference citations that could be a temperature gauge as to the veracity of the book in question. The scientific and other published documentation that an author includes at the back of the book is good form, since it gives credibility to what he/she writes.

Jake Page's book checked out fine in this respect, and when I saw his appendices I felt that this was a healthy cat book, not stuffed with fluff and nonsense. Some cat books, like many cats, are warm and fuzzy but actually quite boring, or worse, rather sickly, not put together well and soon to be buried and forgotten. Yet others are highly inbred, copycat books, inferior rip-offs of better originals. A few make a lifetime's impression.

I have known a few cool cats like that, and this book is one of which they would certainly not disapprove.

I sensed Page's love and concern for cats, clearly evident in the appendices that draw attention to the epidemic of nutrition-related disease linked to feeding cats manufactured pet food, especially the dry kibble types. I was glad to see him focus on the most common ailments in the various purebreds, some of which may be hereditary—an increasing problem—or linked to breed sensitivities to certain food ingredients, antiflea and other veterinary drugs, anesthetics, and vaccines.

So I felt that further examination of this book was called for. Like opening a cat's mouth, I wasn't sure what I might find when I scanned the contents and began to sniff out the introduction. Would it bite and grab my attention?

Catchy titles aside, the introduction was like being greeted by my cat Igor when I come home from work. I felt the immediate embrace of a kindred spirit dedicated to the task of helping people better understand the nature of animals, and the animals of nature. What better way for us to see, or at least get a better glimpse of, the cats' world than through their eyes?

Satisfied and encouraged by the introduction, I stalked through the book swiftly, enjoying it, and then returned to savor the heart and marrow of each chapter like a big cat who first surveys the herd of wildebeest or antelope before deciding where to start first.

From the first chapter on I was captivated and appreciative of Page's accumulated and well-integrated natural history knowledge. Thanks to writers like him, the often painstaking and patience-demanding observations of ethologists—scientists who study the ethos/behavior of fellow creatures, and whose findings, along with those of other natural scientists, are too often buried and forgotten in academic journals—are rescued and shared with a wider readership.

People's attitudes toward cats vacillate between revulsion and reverence, fear and kinship, from age to age and individual to individual. Cats, as you will read, have been victims of human prejudice and cruelties based primarily on ignorance and indifference for centuries. This book is an antidote and will do much to further people's acceptance and enjoyment of cats. It is also an antidote to cats being victims of misperception and misunderstanding that can cause them to be overindulged, inappropriately disciplined, or otherwise mistreated; and to be so highly anthropomorphized as to be regarded and treated like infant children or surrogate offspring rather than as cats with their own special nature, ethos, spirit.

I was hoping to see some mention of the psychic and spiritual aspects of cat mythology and phenomenology so as to compare my findings and conclusions with the author's. This is not within the scope of feline natural history, however, so I respectfully refer the reader to my own work, *Cat Body, Cat Mind.* As a scientist I became intrigued when many years ago a reader of my syndicated newspaper column, *Animal Doctor,* told me of the family cat who suddenly began to pace and cry in evident distress one morning around ten. Then, around 11:00 a.m., the veterinary hospital called to say that the family's beloved dog, which was very closely bonded with the cat, had expired on the operating table at around 10 a.m. Somehow the cat seemed to know when her beloved canine companion had passed on. But how? Over the years I have collected many such anecdotes, and they do make one wonder about the awareness and sensitivities of other creatures, and our own limited senses.

Scientific studies of feline behavioral genetics and the almost

ephemeral, matrifocal, littercentric social psyche and ethos of the domestic cat are usefully summarized in this book. You will learn about the sociability of cats, and the feral cat "societies" that congregate around garbage dumps and warehouses. A common contemporary prejudice toward cats is over the free-roaming cats' predatory behavior, killing and maiming song-birds and other wildlife. Others put food out for such homeless cats, or see nothing wrong with allowing their own cats to roam free and hunt and kill. Importantly this bioethical controversy—kill them or feed them, trap and adopt them, or spay-neuter-vaccinate and release them—is laid out in this book. It makes for a good foundation for conflict resolution between the polarized extremes of cat lovers and protectors and cat haters and exterminators.

Rather than being another sentimental celebration of cats, *Do Cats Hear With Their Feet?* provides the knowledge and insights to better our appreciation, understanding, care, and concern for all cats great and small—and the promise of a more fulfilling relationship and communion with those felines who enrich our personal lives. A gift indeed.

Dr. Michael W. Fox
Author of *Cat Body, Cat Mind*

DO
CATS
HEAR
WITH THEIR
FEET?

Figgy watches cat TV.

INTRODUCTION

Her golden eyes
Gaze upon
Silken chocolate
Her whiskers
Are aristocratic lace
She surveys
Flurried winds
In the grass below her
And settles more comfortably
On the provided fence
The sun bestows its luster
On her rippling fur coat
And if, perhaps, a clumsy horse
Should amble by,
Le Chat
Will only flick an ear
With elegant
Disdain

—NINA KUNTZ

From the young Montana poet above to the Egyptian priests of the time of the pharaohs, people have sung of cats, seeking to fix in our minds (or at least theirs) the myriad facets of that familiar but enigmatic creation of nature and mankind. Being neither poet nor priest, I have resorted to a rather comfortable and old-fashioned mode—natural history—to shed some light on cats, the most popular pets in the United States with numbers ranging in the eighty millions, and by other estimates accounting for approximately one-fourth of the 400-odd million pet cats in the world.

Natural history is a courteous form of inquiry that asks where a given creature came from, how it lives its life, and what it can do for us, at the same time asking what we can do for it. Natural history typically looks at the whole animal, rather than its intimate chemistry, and asks how it gets along in its environment. Of course, in these days of the unveiling of the genetic code of humans, dogs, mice, and cats (among others), and of the cloning of sheep and, one supposes, humans before long, as well as high-tech genetic engineering capable of creating a cat that glows in the dark with an eerie reddish light, natural history needs to open its old hand-carved oaken doors of knowledge and allow the shiny titanium of DNA labs into its old precincts—but not so far in as to be confusing. Natural history also looks at bones that have turned to stone—fossils—to fill in the long story of life on this earth, and we will peer at a few of those in passing.

Contemplating this grand old field of study, I consulted (for courage if nothing else) a book first published in 1950 and still in print, *The Nature of Natural History*, by Marston Bates. Bates was a professor of biology when I met him in the late 1960s who held a weekly seminar in his house called "Biology and Human Affairs," lubricated with copious free beer and touching on topics too numerous to list. He also had added to the back of his house a large greenhouse that contained an amazing array of tropical life forms—plants, of course, and animals ranging from monkeys to exotic birds, including a hummingbird who insisted on checking out every visitor close up as they came through the beaded curtains into the greenhouse. This installation was what Bates wrote about in *Natural History* magazine, and later in a book of the same name, as a "jungle in the house." It is the reason, at least indirectly, that my wife Susanne and I, hosts to multiple dogs, chickens, guinea pigs, and bearded dragons, no longer can have cats inside the house. (We do help support a number of feral cats who patrol the small agricultural valley where we live.)

To build a jungle in one's house calls for patience. Tropical forests, no matter how small, do not come about overnight. We began in the 1970s with a home-built flight cage into which we introduced a few pairs of tropical finches and a bunch of ferns. Monkeys, after all, are a bit hard to come by and harder yet to manage. We soon noticed that the finches liked to tear pieces of fern off and leave them lying around, so we experimented with other plants. I also noticed that the finches, regardless of what species they were, reproduced with startling, almost unseemly rapidity, creating new pairs of new and different species and colors. While I pondered this biological anomaly, Susanne (who I suspected had something to do with the anomaly) began to plan the conversion of a side porch into a full-fledged ecosystem, with small trees, gardenia plants, a waterfall with a pond housing the turtles that already inhabited an aquarium in the

kitchen, and plenty more finches of varying colors and behaviors. In all, we would eventually wind up with some twenty-eight finches and waxbills, button quail, turtles (of course), and a lot of uninvited mice. Eventually cardinals, beset by winter snows, looked in enviously at these equally colorful denizens in their hot humid world.

But in our jungle's infant stage, we began to notice that the flight cage was not only adding pairs of other species but losing the occasional singleton. We had strung the front of the cage with piano wire, just as they did in exhibits at the National Zoo, the idea being that the piano wire was almost invisible because it was highly unreflective. We failed to notice (at first) that the piano wire did not remain taut, though it looked taut.

We soon discovered that the missing finches were being caught at night by a member of our household known familiarly as Figgy, or more formally as Fig Newton. Figgy was, of course, a cat. To be particular, a Chinchilla Persian, mostly gray and utterly friendly to the human members of the household, which included at least six teenagers at any given time.

Figgy, a gift to us, was smart enough to reach a paw through the vertical strands of piano wire and fetch unwary finches. On the other hand, Figgy seemed to lack a certain understanding of personal safety. He spent a lot of each day sleeping in the street outside our house, which was located in Washington, D.C. He was run over and lost a rear leg, but persisted in lying in the street and got hit again, this time without loss of limb. He was not much interested in mice. We realized that however hampered he may have been by being a tripod, and not a very smart tripod, he was a clever and highly successful predator of expensive tropical finches. And so, sadly, reluctantly, but necessarily, we handed Figgy off to a friend—a very proper fellow with daughters who wouldn't ever have dreamed of keeping birds in his house.

That was long ago. Even earlier, we had hosted an orange Persian named Rudolph whom the reader will meet later and who was stolen by a man of God. By the time the topic of this book came up, Susanne and I had already produced one book about the natural history of dogs, which had accumulated to a full half-dozen in our house while the great avian empire had dwindled to naught as empires often do. Wistfully we went to the local humane society and looked at the (mostly) tabbies seeking a home. The lady there, upon hearing about our dogs, discouraged us from taking a cat home, the assumption being that if it were to run away, it would be—simply—curtains. So this book draws upon old memories and some stories supplied by friends that, I hope, illustrate in a pleasing way some of the amazing things about cats that science—in the form of natural historians (and, yes, a few molecular types)—has discovered about these remarkable animals, the last animals on earth to be domesticated . . . if indeed they have been.

This book, then, is about how some strange little weasel-like animals living forty million years ago came to be felines, how one of them recently came to live with us humans, how we have viewed these companions through the millennia, and what we know about how their minds work. Or to put it another way, what they appear to think about us.

PART ONE
TRANSFORMATIONS

We include signposts along the route to becoming feline,

detour briefly into the world of the saber-tooths, meet

the one species of wild cat who came to be domesticated,

find where and when it probably took place, and

examine some of the ways the idea of the cat has

been applied to the dreams, bugaboos, and goals

of humankind, even today.

MARY'S CRICKET IS PERIPHERALLY OBSERVING THE PHOTOGRAPHER.

1

Just-So Tales of Cat Beginnings

But I tell you, a cat needs a name that's particular,
A name that's peculiar, and more dignified,
Else how can he keep up his tail perpendicular.
Or spread out his whiskers, or cherish his pride?

—T. S. ELIOT

I am not in any position to argue with T. S. Eliot, so we must begin this long contemplation of the cat by looking at names, specifically scientific names. For some people, the names that scientists assign to animals and plants are a pain in the neck to remember, being made up of two words (at least) and expressed in a kind of Greco-Latin mongrel language that is hard to pronounce or remember and that begs translation. This is done for purposes of precision, not to exclude laymen from the priesthood. Also, scientific names are kind of backward. The last name says what species the animal is, and the first name refers to the genus (plural: genera), which is the group of species to which this animal is closely related. If the logic of these scientific names were applied to me, for example, and in English, my name would be Page Jake. Either way, the name is particular if not peculiar and that is the point of scientific names.

The name that science has bequeathed the domestic cat is not as peculiar as Eliot's Quaxo, or Rumpelteazer, or Macavity, but it is highly specific, even what might be called particular: *Felis catus*. It means "Cat cat," which is to say the species "cat" in the genus "Cat." Most emphatically, then, *Felis catus* is a cat. The name was bestowed by Carl von Linne, a Swedish biologist otherwise known as Linnaeus, who in the eighteenth century developed the two-name, or binomial, system of naming all God's creatures. The name, while particular, does not match in any way the lithe grace, the nonchalance, or the sleek mystery of the cat, but one learns not to expect poetry from science in such matters.

Until recently the scientists (called taxonomists) who continued Linnaeus's work had a pretty straightforward and simple way of naming all the cats in the world. They put all but one into two large groups based chiefly on size. All the big cats—charismatic megafauna, they are sometimes called: lions, tigers, jaguars, leopards, and so forth—were placed in the genus *Panthera*. One thing the pantherine cats have in common is a small cartilaginous doodad called a hyoid in the throat that, along with other features, allows them to roar.

All but one of the other cats were put into the genus *Felis*. Among the felines, the hyoid doodad is bony, not soft, and they cannot roar. The exception was the cheetah. It inhabited a third genus, namely *Acinonyx*, all by itself. The reason for this exclusion is that cheetahs have proportionately longer legs than most cats, shorter snouts, bigger nostrils, more domed heads, a more flexible backbone, and feet without retractable claws. All of those features (except maybe the domed head) combine to make the cheetah the world's greatest short-distance sprinter, clocked at around seventy miles an hour when chasing down a Thomson's gazelle over some 400 yards.

All the other cats, large and small, pantherine and feline (and in all there are some thirty-six species by some ways of counting), are built to be hunters who sneak up on their prey, run it down in a short burst of speed, and dispatch it before quickly eating it. (Well, there are exceptions to all rules: a house cat will sometimes bat a captured mouse around for a while before eating it, and many wild cats will eat some and cache the rest for later.) Overall, this sets the cats apart from the cheetah and its amazing velocity, and from wild dogs like wolves that tear at the prey animal during the chase.

Cats, using the term inclusively here, seem from the very beginnings of catdom long ago in a nearly unimaginably distant past to have hit upon the largely ideal physique for their kind of work. As British paleontologist Alan Turner writes, structurally the domestic cat "can be seen as simply a scaled-down version of a lion or a leopard, and in evolutionary terms the larger cats may even be considered as scaled-up versions of something much like a domestic cat." They all have relatively long limbs, a short gut for digesting only meat, feet with claws (all but the cheetah's being retractable), scissorlike cheek teeth called carnassials for shearing off pieces of meat, and especially long, sharp canine teeth. They are extremely supple animals, and most of them can climb trees with ease, though many don't bother. In any event, the resemblance of one cat to another is great. Cats are all recognizably cats. By contrast there are dogs that look like fat mongooses, raccoons, and powder puffs; see, for example, the Shih Tzu.

It seems a shame then, to me at least, that the Felid Taxon

Advisory Group and others involved in cat taxonomy have recently chosen to add a host of new genus names and species names to further differentiate cats even though they are all so much alike. This happens periodically in taxonomy. For a while the "splitters" get the upper hand and genus and species names proliferate, cats that are separated only by geography getting to be separate species. And what with modern genetics, scientists can pinpoint almost infinitesimally small differences that make splitting almost irresistible. But usually the "lumpers" take over after a while and put everything back together again. A complete list of this riotous profusion of cat names can be found in appendix A, which is a brief catalogue of all the wild cats.

There used to be an almost hard-and-fast, and practical, rule about the idea of a species. It was simply that all members of a species can breed with each other but cannot successfully breed with members of another species and produce reproductively viable offspring (meaning grandchildren). Mate a horse with a donkey and you get a mule that is sterile. End of lineage.

But for a long time now, the wild dogs have messed this all up. Coyotes, wolves, domestic dogs, and so forth were all given their own binomial names, *Canis lupus* for wolves, *Canis latrans* for coyotes, and *Canis familiaris* for the domestic dog. But they can all successfully mate and produce viable offspring. In fact, they are all one species that has the capacity to house a lot of variation. And it is now the same with cats. Some rather intrusive people have mated lions and tigers and leopards in various combinations, producing ligers, tiglons, and leopons—and some combinations and particularly females have produced sexually viable offspring.

These brave new feline hybrids are confined chiefly, and one

might say mercifully, to some zoos and animal parks, but consider the Savannah cat, one of several wild cats recently turned
into breeds of domestic cat for cat shows and as pets. The Savannah is the product (originally) of a regular house cat of one
type or another and a wild serval. Servals are wild African cats
larger than house cats, brightly spotted black on tawny, long-
legged (to see over savannah grasses), large-eared, and totally
elegant. It might be a bit alarming to those who feed birds in
winter to know the serval can leap ten feet into the air to snatch
a passing bird. The serval's binomial name is now *Leptailurus
serval,* meaning small deer-cat, which of course makes no sense
whatsoever, especially since deer don't live in Africa, and there
are a number of wild cat species smaller than the serval. Scientific names are highly particular but often peculiarly undescrip-
tive—even unapt. In any event, a number of cat fanciers in the
United States and abroad raise this new hybrid, the Savannah
cat, for sale, claiming that particularly after a couple of generations mated to house cats it becomes altogether friendly, calm,
and safe, all the while retaining its spectacular serval markings.
But here, I complain, we are given an entirely new *genus* than
Felis, and an entirely new *species* than *catus* for a big-eared, spotted cat that can without much ado mate with the domestic cat
and produce yet another sort of do-
mestic cat. This seems to me splitting gone seriously awry.

The reader may have noticed
that I am on the side of lumpers. I am
also mildly suspicious of domestic-wild
hybrids. I worry that the serval lurking
in the Savannah cat might one day look

at its human admirer and revert to the wild. This is just what wolf-dog hybrids do quite frequently.

Further proof of why the shape and workings of the essential cat are so apt for its job of surviving as a prey-catching, meat-eating mammal (called an obligate carnivore: no veggies or fruits) is that this anatomical pattern has essentially come into being at least two other times—in the deep past and in Australia. Australia is, of course, a very strange place with an odd accent and where virtually no placental mammals ever evolved. Some arrived later, brought along by people. But before that there were effectively only marsupials, mammals that kept their infant offspring (in essence, fetuses) in a pouch, the most familiar of which are the kangaroo and the koala. A handful of egg-laying mammals, called monotremes, exist as well, the most familiar of which is the duck-billed platypus. In Australia there were a great variety of ecological niches, most of them comparable to niches in the rest of the world. Large kangaroos, for example, provided a niche for a good-sized carnivore to chase down, and evolution provided a very catlike array of big marsupial predators including a marsupial "lion" and also a marsupial dead ringer (well, almost) for a saber-tooth cat. The marsupial lion is of special interest to scientists. Called *Thylacoleo carnifex*, which translates to "marsupial executioner," it was surely the most ferocious animal ever to grace the shores of Australia. Hugely powerful, with forelegs twice the thickness of a leopard's, this 250-pound predator had an Australian version of the shearing cheek teeth called carnassials that most carnivores possess, except that these were especially large. Its canines were just stubs, but its front (incisor) teeth were exceedingly sharp. Its jaws and teeth have been described as "bolt cutters," and it killed its prey—thought to include three-ton wombats—with a sudden devastating scissorlike bite that inflicted instant death. Related to the wombats, as are koalas and kangaroos, it seems to have gone extinct sometime about 30,000 years ago (thank heavens, one might say).

Australia saw the rise, as well, of marsupial versions of practically all the families of placental mammals, a process called convergent evolution in which, at different times and/or places, similar niches or jobs call for similar actors.

Second, and largely contemporaneous with the rise of the earliest cats, was another family of predators called nimravids that looked like cats and acted like cats but weren't cats. Some speculate that the nimravids may have sprung from some dog-like ancestor and evolved into a highly catlike form. The fossil record is just too sparse to be sure of any of this. The nimravids too developed long legs with claws on the feet, a shortening of the face, slicing cheek teeth, and big sharp canines. Some of them grew long, flat, and curved canines like the saber-tooths.

NIMRAVID
BARBOUROFELIS
MORRISI

But a tiny difference that only a paleontologist would see as important distinguished the nimravids from the true cats. The difference lay in a tiny organ called the auditory bulla, which is a capsule that houses the little bones that connect the eardrum to the inner ear. In cats this capsule still is mostly bone, while it was only cartilaginous in the nimravids. It couldn't have been this feature alone that actually kept the two families separate while plying much the same niche for millions of years, but

such is all the evidence the paleontologist often has. Over time
the nimravid lineage produced more than six genera, and they
died out some five million years ago, causes unknown, after a
successful run of about thirty million years on the planetary
stage.

What is clear from all this reverting to a type is that the earth
has long cried out for catlike predators. How long, in fact?

The last of the dinosaurs left the earthly plane about sixty-
three million years ago, and scientists have long thought that
their demise allowed the mammals—tiny creatures that lived
in the shadow of the reptilian lords of the earth, surviving on
insects—to grow in number, kind, and size and, with hot-
blooded alacrity, take over. In fact, some dog-sized mammals
shared the planet in the last few dinosaurian eras, but most
were smaller than dogs and most of the surviving mammals
stayed pretty small for some twenty million post-dinosaurian
years. At this point—about forty million years ago—there
appears to have been a great change in the earth's atmosphere, in
particular a huge growth in the amount of available oxygen. The
percentage of oxygen rose from 10 percent in dinosaurian times
to 23 percent forty million years ago (that's a bit more oxygen
than we live on). Some speculate that it was this huge increase in
available oxygen that permitted some mammals to grow larger,
eventually providing the planet with the likes of twelve-foot tall
sloths, enormous cave bears, a rhinoceros approximately the size
of a two-story garage, and huge saber-tooth cats.

In any event, by forty million years ago it was noticeably the
mammals' world and various sorts inhabited all the old dino-
saur niches. Among these were the miacids—arboreal animals
something like weasels. One branch of miacids gave rise to the

doglike lineages, including
bears (which came later),
and it may have been
another miacid line that
gave rise to those ani-
mals that would *resemble*

MIACID

cats on the one hand (the nimravids), and those that actually
became cats on the other. But this is all a bit murky.

The first known catlike creature, a nimravid, arose about
thirty-six million years ago, and the first true cats arose six
million years after the nimravids appeared. Thereafter, early
cat evolution is all pretty opaque given the likelihood that most
of these protocats got under way in wet if not tropical forests
where animal remains rarely become fossilized.

The creature that gets the nod as First Cat looked something
like a weasel and was adept at leaping from branch to branch in
trees. Its skull was more like that of a cat than a weasel, however,
and its teeth were also catlike though it had more teeth than the
thirty cats usually have. It is called *Proailurus lemanensis*, the

word *ailurus* being bowd-
lerized from the Greek for
cat. The fossil of this creature was found in France,

PROAILURUS

dating from thirty million years ago.
The sparseness of cat fossils is
made all the clearer by the fact
that the next *Proailurus* fossil to
be found was in Nebraska, dating from sixteen million years
ago. Not much had changed in all that time, suggesting that this
animal was very well adjusted to the environments of the times.

Fourteen million years is a long time to be pretty much the same animal—if indeed it really remained the same through that long period. The vertebral column of this earliest of true cats has never been recovered, so reconstruction of *Proailurus* depends on fossils of the creature that apparently arose next, around twenty million years ago: *Pseudaelurus lorteti.*

Looking at the fossil remnants of this creature one might well mistake them for the skeleton of a modern lynx or a diminutive puma. The main difference was a longer backbone than modern cats typically have and a shorter distance between the feet and the "heel," which is essentially our wrist. At the same time, *Pseudaelurus* would be difficult for a layman to distinguish from *Proailurus.* All this suggests that *Pseudaelurus* was still chiefly a tree-dweller. It was (at a great remove and via various unknown descendants) the progenitor of both the true cats and those scary, bizarre, and controversial saber-tooth cats, the first of which we know from some twelve million years ago. Indeed, it seems that the saber-tooth cats got the jump on the familiar true cats by some two or three million years.

We will pause here briefly on the trail of *Felis catus* to ponder these terrifying killers of old that some people insist on calling saber-tooth *tigers,* which they weren't. Tigers were the last of the big pantherine cats to evolve. The saber-tooths were a wholly separate branch of catlike creatures from the true cats, including the tigers and lions and house cats. While they were, in fact, more lionlike than anything else, it is pretty sure they would not have been able to breed with anything but other saber-tooths. In all, there were at least six different genera of these monsters, only two genera of which were still present in what is called recent times, beginning some 20,000 years ago at the

approximate end of the last Ice Age. The last of all to survive
was the genus *Smilodon* of the western hemisphere. All
of the saber-tooths (except *Smilodon*) had developed a
flange at the bottom of the lower jaw against which the
enlarged canine teeth rested. Possibly this flange lying
against the prey provided a firm base of sorts for the en-
suing bite. Or perhaps not.

The saber-tooth cats were all robust, but the South American species of *Smilodon*, called *Smilodon populator*, was one
of the biggest, a brawny creature that might better have been
called *Smilodon DEpopulator*. Its forelimbs were so strong they
made the hind limbs look weak. Most likely they preyed with
deadly efficiency on giant sloths and other slow-moving plant
eaters, grabbing prey with their hugely powerful forelegs and
knocking it to the ground, immobilizing it before delivering the
coup de grace. By comparison, the most familiar saber-tooth cat
is the much smaller lion-sized *Smilodon fatalis*. It has turned
up in great numbers in the La Brea Tar Pits in downtown Los
Angeles, where thousands of late Pleistocene predators became
trapped (and preserved) while trying to grab on to prey that had
also gotten stuck. These cats were lion-sized but brawnier than
today's lions.

SMILODON FATALIS SKULL AND RECONSTRUCTION

To hold up close a skull of one of these predators, as I did
once in the home of a California fossil collector, and to touch
the awesome canines, dark and shiny, was enough to make me
shudder. The species name, *fatalis*, seems altogether apt: what
could be more terrifyingly lethal than to see that gaping maw
a split-second away, two eight-inch saberlike fangs about to be
sunk into your . . .

But no.

All the saber-tooths had jaws that could open to a tremendous angle, permitting the two great saberlike canines to function—but just how they functioned has puzzled paleontologists for a long time, as we shall see.

Suggestions about those big teeth have been many, ranging from use as a kind of can opener of highly armored animals like the giant glyptodont relatives of armadillos, to mollusk openers something like an oyster shucker's knife, to (altogether outlandishly) tree-climbing aids. The long-accepted notion of how these enormously elongated canine teeth were used is to be seen in many old illustrations: the cat sinks its knifelike fangs into the prey animal's neck or flank, stabbing down like we would use a sharp steel hunting knife.

It turns out that some Australian scientists have muscled into the study of one of America's most charismatic fauna and shown to their satisfaction that for all the hardware, *Smilodon*'s jaw muscles were not very strong. And another thing, says Britain's Alan Turner: "almost the slightest movement on the part of the struggling prey would have threatened breakage in such circumstances." Not only that, but those fangs were nowhere near as sharp as a steel knife and it would probably have taken far more force than these giant cats could have mustered to sink them all the way into a victim's flesh. Also, it is possible that, in such a scenario, the lower jaw would get in the way (though some paleontologists deny that). The coup de grace to the standard explanation is that, in most saber-tooth fossil remains, the big canines are typically less worn down than all the other teeth, meaning that their use was relatively limited.

So when were they used and for what? An American paleontologist, William Akersten, has suggested that when one of these cats (or perhaps several) went after large prey such as a juvenile mammoth, they would use the canines to take a shearing bite, say, in the abdomen, once the animal was pretty much immobilized by the cat's powerful forelimbs and claws. The canines would pierce slightly in and then across the belly, with the lower jaw biting upward to help create a gaping wound that caused great blood loss and shock. The cats could then simply sit back and wait for the animal to die and the feast to begin.

However they used those teeth, the African saber-tooths' final two or three million years on the planet were shared with bipedal mammals on their way to becoming human. One can hardly doubt that the presence of these terrifying predators in the landscape had something to do with calling forth the increasing braininess of our ancestors. Avoiding those huge teeth would have been a major challenge to the diminutive (four feet tall) *Homo habilis* and only the wily and careful among them would have survived long enough to have produced modern humanity including, among others, paleontologists and cat lovers.

A persistent myth had it that *Smilodon fatalis* went extinct when its huge canines grew so large that the poor creature could not open (or close) its mouth. That is, of course, nonsense. Like most of the other large predators of the North American ice-age landscape, the saber-tooths went extinct when their large and slow-moving mammalian prey went extinct, almost surely the result of rapid climatic and environmental upheavals brought about by the receding of the great glaciers.

The coming and going of glaciers would also play a major role in the whereabouts of today's cats, mainly by raising or lowering the sea level, which in turn destroyed or created land bridges between Asia and Alaska, North and South America, and various other places around the globe.

While the saber-tooths were still onstage, the feline branch

was also churning out a few relatively minor variations on the cat theme, the greatest variant of which was the giant cheetahs that arose in North America and some three million years ago migrated over the Bering land bridge into Asia and Africa. The phrase "land bridge" suggests a narrow isthmus at best, but in fact when the seas receded periodically, sucked up by glaciers, it exposed a hunk of land between Siberia and Alaska that was about a thousand miles wide, a splendid avenue for the interchange of Asian and American animals. Cheetahs seem to be the only great cats to have arisen in North America and migrated to Asia and thence to Africa. All the other big cats got their start in the Old World and came to the New World via Beringia, as it is sometimes called. Meanwhile horses and camels, for example, arose in the Americas and used the two-way street to go to Asia.

Eventually the cheetahs of North America went extinct, leaving the ball game to now-smaller cheetahs in Africa and the Middle East. No one seems to know exactly where the first cheetahs—those big ones in North America—came from. Some scientists have speculated that they were actually offshoots of the puma or mountain lion, the ancestors of which arose here about three million years ago. The mountain lions, however, are not accorded a taxonomic invitation into the superstars of catdom, the roaring pantherines, but are instead classed as the biggest of the felines. The mountain lions along with lynxes and ocelots all arose from Old World progenitors, arriving in North America via the Bering land bridge.

MOUNTAIN
LION

I am often made aware of

some of this evolutionary creation—namely, the mountain lions. Several of them live in the open lands around my house and in the hills and mountains beyond. And part of the territory of several of them happens to include the town I live next to in a little valley. One of them was seen strolling past the elementary school one morning about an hour before all the children showed up, and there have been many sightings in the town itself. Here, the mountain lion uses the dirt road I live on as part of his (or her) regular beat, and has been seen a few feet from our house by numerous visitors. His or her tracks adorn the snow.

A great debate is carried out about these lions in this part of Colorado, with many people saying that they were here before we were and therefore must be afforded space for their livelihoods. There are also plenty who suggest that the lions' livelihood, when allowed near or in towns, can include people's cats and dogs, not to mention the occasional human child, and so some sort of control is called for. But what control? The county is dead set against allowing the hunting of these magnificent animals, but without hunting, the big cats become utterly fearless of human habitations. The policy is also a bit two-faced or, if you wish, it has a double standard. If a bear appears in town, it is darted with an anesthetic, tagged on the ear, and taken elsewhere. If that same bear turns up in town again, the wildlife people shoot it. Bears practically never bother people, but mountain lions often do. Mountain lions are thought by some as ghostly, so careful are they to avoid being seen. But the lions here have a new psychology: I don't know anyone in my town who hasn't seen one of them. Yet no one is empowered to dart and tag a mountain lion, and shoot it if it turns up again. Fierce emotion smothers both sides of the mountain lion issue here-

abouts and in many other western states, and no reasonable resolution of it is anywhere in sight. Until magically the solution appears, one is advised never to walk around here alone.

Lions—giant ones ancestral to the African and Asian lions of today—appear to have arisen in Africa some two million or so years ago and began spreading out from Africa about 700,000 years ago. By 250,000 years ago they had spread into Europe and Asia. From there they reached into the Americas as far south as Peru. Indeed, at this time lions lived on five continents, perhaps the greatest range for a wild animal in the history of the planet. But then with the warming up of the climate as a result of the retreat of the last great glaciation beginning some 20,000 years ago, the lions of the world declined to southwestern Asia, India, and Africa, and the cheetahs died out in their original home, retreating to Africa and southwestern Asia.

The other great predators—leopards—began their career in India some six and a half million years ago, spreading into Africa and southern and eastern Asia. The early ones resembled today's jaguars in that they were brawnier, perhaps better suited to life in the forests. The jaguars evolved from Asian leopard progenitors and spread to the Americas about two million years ago. During the ice ages of the late Pleistocene, jaguars decreased in size with shorter legs as open prairies were replaced by forest. Two million years ago, a small version of the tiger lived in southeastern Asia and spread quite rapidly throughout much of Asia within a million years.

My wife Susanne and I saw one of the first footprints of a jaguar to appear in the United States in about a hundred years. We were on mules in the Peloncillo Mountains that lie across the New Mexico–Arizona border and abut the Mexican border. We were following Warner Glenn, a fourth-generation Arizona rancher in the Borderlands and a well-known mountain lion hunter and guide. (I confess I think wistfully of Warner every time the mountain lion turns up in our yard.) He also spotted a male jaguar in the Peloncillos a few years back, photographed it when it was "treed" in the rocks, and used the photographs to start a fund to pay any rancher if he could prove his livestock was killed by the jaguar, the first one to enter the United States in a century. Typically when a Western rancher sees something like that, the rule is Shoot, Shovel, and Shut Up. But Warner wanted people to know that the ranchers had been taking good enough care of the lands they grazed that jaguars felt okay coming back.

At one point, he asked Susanne to dismount and photograph a fresh cat footprint in the mud near a spring. She dismounted and did his bidding; we thought it was the footprint of a mountain lion. Months later, we sent Warner a print of the photograph; he told us that it was the print of a female jaguar, not a mountain lion. So there was a pair of jaguars in the United States after all that time.

JAGUAR FRONT FOOT (LEFT), LION FRONT FOOT (RIGHT)

Over the millennia, the world filled up with great cats. Even more populous, however, in range, size, and variety—if less charismatic—were the smaller feline strains, few of which left much by way of fossil remains. These are the ocelots, jaguarundis, jungle cats, margays, servals, lynxes, and others, all of which were minor variations on the general theme of cat. Indeed, except for changes in size, cat evolution had essentially come to a (presumably comfortable) end. No extravagant

changes were called for anymore: cats as constituted could go practically anywhere they wanted to.

The lynx lineage arose four million years ago in Africa, reaching Asia, Europe, and eventually, a mere 200,000 years ago, the Americas. The North American lynx soon gave rise to the bobcat, one of whose descendants often leaves a trail of footprints through my yard in the winter snows. Unlike the local mountain lion(s), I have never seen this bobcat, being an obligate day person while the bobcat is a night owl. It is only a ghostly presence on the periphery of my life.

It needs to be pointed out that the times and even places for the evolution of all these different sorts of cats is ever subject to revision, especially by genetic analysis, and may or may not turn out to match what little we do know from the sparse fossil record. So far the geneticists and the paleontologists seem to be in overall agreement, but I am confident that even as I write those words, a squabble is brewing. Indeed, most of the smaller cats are known by as little as a few lower jaws, which isn't a whole lot to go on even for the most astute paleontological Sherlocks.

Now, however, it is time to look more closely at one of these lesser known feline species, the wild cat of the woods, or *Felis silvestris*. More to the point, we must look at *Felis silvestris lybica*, otherwise called the African wild cat (and also called the Near Eastern wild cat and the Egyptian wild cat), a little-known creature just a bit larger than that most emphatically catlike cat, *Felis catus*. For the genes of the African wild cat are to be found in every one of the untold millions of domesticated cats that now inhabit the planet. And indeed, many of the few taxonomists who concern themselves with cats now refer to domesticated cats with the longer and slightly more euphonious phrase, *Felis silvestris catus.* But that also assigns the domestic cat the less exalted status of a mere subspecies of *Felis silvestris,* and to this development, a perfectly arbitrary demotion in my view, given the taxonomic murk that has been visited upon the feline family, I would expect cat lovers to strenuously, vocally object.

FERAL CAT LEAVES OLD SHED, PHOTOGRAPHED BY A MOTION-SENSITIVE CAMERA
YET TO CATCH A MOUNTAIN LION.

Chapter 2
The Taming of the Cat

The wildcat is the "real" cat, the soul of the domestic cat; unknowable to human beings, he yet exists inside our household pets, who have long ago seduced us with their seemingly civilized ways.

—JOYCE CAROL OATES

In the year 2006, archaeologists found a grave on the Mediterranean island of Cyprus that contained the remains of a human male and a cat. The grave dated back some 9,500 years. Only shortly before this time, some 14,000 or so years ago, people had begun to settle down in permanent villages in what we now think of as Greece, Turkey, and the Middle East and grow a lot of their food—wheat, barley, and so forth. This created a new ecological niche in the world—a storehouse of fresh grain. Nature may abhor a vacuum, but Nature gets giddy with delight at a new ecological niche. Food for mice, rats, and other rodents could now be found in concentrated areas called granaries, and they quickly found their way into these somewhat leaky cornucopias, some of them becoming a new species—the house mouse, for example, which is by now probably the most widespread mammal on earth besides *Homo sapiens*. Anyway, the rodents were, of course, followed by wild cats, for whom the concentration of prey was also something of a bonanza.

Some wild cats would then, over generations, become accustomed to the presence of humans (and humans to the presence of the cats) and thus from the helpful raiders of pestilential rodents the domestic cat would have emerged. So the story goes, and it is probably true in a general way, but of course it couldn't have been quite that simple.

Most of the few scientists who concern themselves with the domestication of cats do not, for example, believe that the 9,500-year-old grave on Cyprus represents the earliest known example of *Felis catus*. Instead, it probably represents a wild cat that had been tamed somewhere and brought to the island, presumably by its dead friend. There is no record of any wild cats having inhabited Cyprus before this time. Yet another Cyprus grave, dated to about 9,000 years ago, also contained a human and a cat, along with such grave goods as polished stones, jewelry, and tools, but again it appears that the cat (its remains telling us it was the size of a small wild cat of the Mediterranean region) was not fully domesticated, though it could have been a pet of some sort. Besides arguments among paleontologists, this series of assertions also raises the awkward question of the difference between being tamed and being domesticated.

You can take the kitten of a Bengal tiger and arduously raise it by hand (pretty much a full-time job) and maybe have yourself a tame adult tiger—at least for a while. There is no guarantee that your tamed young tiger will remain tame when it reaches full adulthood. And if your tame tiger breeds with another tame tiger, the offspring will not likely be tame. You will need to start over again. The process of domestication, on the other hand, produces certain psychological alterations along with physical ones, and in the extreme renders the domesticated creatures largely incapable of surviving without human intervention.

An example of this kind of total domestication is corn, which started out in the wild as a kind of grass with a loose clump of little seeds on the tip of its stem. As humans began planting the seeds and choosing to harvest the plants with the biggest seeds, the seeds became larger, more tightly packed, and, incidentally, less likely to be blown off the stalk or to fall off. In other words, humans would have to harvest the kernels and plant them. Otherwise, no corn would grow next year. No domesticated animal is *that* domesticated.

Cats and dogs are the most thoroughly domesticated animals we know of, at least by one fairly straightforward criterion: they are the only domesticated animals that do not need to be fenced in to remain as part of a household. (Of course, as in all such assertions, there are exceptions. Some cats and some dogs simply wander off.) The other all-purpose criterion is that domesticated creatures should not be able to make it on their own in the wild. Unfenced cows, for example, would almost surely wander off and succumb to predators after a short while. Chickens, unpenned at night, soon wind up as owl or coyote food. And so forth. Some dogs might be able to make it in the wild for a while, but feral dogs are known to have much foreshortened life spans. Feral cats, on the other hand, can often find a niche in the country and even in cities where they can thrive in a seedy sort of way, probably for many years. So there are clearly degrees of domestication.

It is in dogs and other canines that scientifically minded folk have most intimately explored the actual processes that occur in the course of an animal becoming domesticated. So briefly we will turn to dogs, the better to understand cats. They are, after all, fellow carnivores.

The general picture of dog domestication is that in the form of

gray wolves they domesticated themselves once humans began to settle down in a permanent or semi-permanent manner some 14,000 to 12,000 years ago or so, and started accumulating garbage in large piles. Some wolves would have begun to feed at these dumps, the naturally tamer (or less fearful) ones making out the best in this new niche, and producing some offspring that were also relatively calm about the presence of humans. It turns out that this increasing tameness would have profound physical and psychological effects. Tails curled up over the back, heads got smaller, pelts became one color or variegated (for example, with white "blazes" against black fur). Genetically—that is, in terms of DNA—there were only the tiniest visible changes, and dogs and wolves remained to all extent and purposes the same. But the timing of the genes' expression changed, so that, for example, the tamer wolves' skulls stopped growing earlier than those of the wild ones (by some four months). Dog skulls are smaller proportionately than wolf skulls. Childish features tended to be retained into adulthood (a process called neoteny). One candidate for what changed the timing of gene expression is slight changes in the rhythm of the pulsing of the thyroid gland, which sends the thyroid hormone into the system, where it essentially controls such things as physical growth and development, fur color, and a host of other features including tooth growth (which led to smaller teeth in dogs).

The emergence of domesticated dogs all seems to have taken place originally in Asia, probably China, some 14,000 or more years ago, and only a few times. Cats, on the other hand, appear to be the last animals to become domesticated, maybe 4,000 years ago. In the interim, cattle, goats, sheep, turkeys, chickens, llamas, horses, and all the other domesticates came about. The only animal to be domesticated since cats were some silver foxes that were bred in a Siberian fur farm by a disgraced Russian scientist who, in the 1950s, had the gall to believe in Mendelian genetics when the Communist Party had its own hopelessly stupid version of genetics invented by a man called Lysenko. The exiled scientist, Dmitry K. Belyaev, began selecting foxes for one trait only—tameness—and within forty generations of increasing tameness, he had produced what amounted to a new kind of dog, the domesticated foxes being fond of humans (though a bit catlike in their occasional bouts of independence) with curled tails, variegated color, smaller heads, and all the other attributes of most domesticated animals. These fox-dogs have not made it much farther into the world at large than their fox farm in Siberia. But the fox dog as a popular breed cannot be far off, for nothing is more appreciated in the world at large, it seems, than novelty.

Presumably, some of the same biological changes came about in the domestication of cats, and we have seen from Belyaev's foxes that the process can occur rather quickly—forty generations of foxes, well within a human life span. Most likely it was faster in Belyaev's case than in the original domestication by wolves, since he was deliberately selecting for tameness from a huge universe of choices, several thousand foxes in all, and also carefully isolating the tamest from the less tame. House cats show many but not all of the same physical traits that arose among the foxes, particularly smaller skulls than wild cats, smaller teeth, great variation in color and patterns of the coat, and a predisposition not to detest or abjectly fear humans. But if wolves were plying Middle Eastern garbage dumps as long ago as 14,000 years, why weren't cats plying the granaries at

that time? Maybe they were and we just don't have any records of it.

On the other hand, you and I (assuming that neither of us are zoologically trained cat experts) would be hard put to tell at a glance the difference between a regular tabby house cat and the wild cat from which the domesticated one arose. That wild progenitor in question is universally taken to be the African wild cat (*Felis silvestris lybica*), one of three main subspecies of wild cat—the African, the European, and the Asian—though these have been yet further broken down into a dizzying array of subspecies. However, the differences are negligible except to a split-minded taxonomist or a fanatical geneticist. They can all mate with each other and heaven knows who else. In any event, the African version of this cat is known to live in every kind of ecosystem on the continent except tropical rain forests and outright deserts, its range stretching through Egypt and into parts of the Middle East. It is clearly a highly adaptable animal. Its coat tends to be lighter in more open, arid lands and darker in forested areas (as with most other cats of the wild). This variation is a response that provides maximum "camouflage" for a cat that depends to a great degree on stealth—which they all do except for lions and cheetahs. Sadly, in virtually all its territory, the wild cat is threatened with an odd sort of extinction—from being interbred out of existence by the domestic cats to whom it gave rise. While it is still among us, we should give it praise. It is responsible for several hundred million cats who live with us on Planet Earth.

FELIS SILVESTRIS LYBICA

At about three feet from stem to tailtip, the African wild cat is a bit larger than the typical house cat, and a bit more robust as well. For reasons that remain mysterious, the African wild cat was more calm or tame or fearless of human interaction, and could give itself over to the process of domestication more readily than the European or Asian wild cat, both of which forcefully resist contact with humans, spitting and howling and carrying on in a totally wild fashion if importuned. Not long ago a zoologist predicted that the domestic cat would have arisen from a wild cat with a proportionately smaller brain, and the African wild cat's brain is indeed a bit smaller than its European and Asian cousins. Another name used for the African wild cat is the Egyptian, and it was generally agreed until 2007 that the ancient Egyptians domesticated the African wild cat.

In that year, a team of geneticists headed by Carlos Driscoll of the U.S. National Cancer Institute announced that the domestic cat was derived from the Near Eastern wild cat (actually a population of the African wild cats) some 10,000 years ago, and the entire planetary realm of house cats and stray cats and feral cats—uncountable millions of them—are the progeny of a mere five female wild cats from the Near East. The study, which took six years to complete, has nothing whatsoever to say about the sires. For now, if you wish, you can imagine a single tom tracking down the five females in heat in his extended territory and becoming one of the most productive male mammals ever to live on the planet. But that is probably not what happened and, indeed, we may never know about the male side of this revolutionary reproductive effort.

The new facts the geneticists have given us are alarming to other scientists called paleontologists, who piece together stories of the past from fragments of fossilized bone along with insights into ancient climates and other scraps of highly circumstantial evidence. When the geneticists breeze in with such

authoritative pronouncements, the noses of the patient sifters of fossils and dirt can get a bit out of joint. Molecular biology is high tech, a hard science within the realm of biology, and a brash newcomer, relatively speaking, in the world of science. Paleontology is, along with the social sciences, generally considered soft science, even though its evidence is as hard as rock and indeed often is just that: rock. (Fossils are bone that is replaced over the eons by rocky minerals.)

The world—and especially the press—likes things that are definite, precise, and easily stated such as: 10,000 years ago, five female Near Eastern wild cats bellied up to the rubbish piles of some settled tribes of agriculturalists and became, or gave rise to, the domestic cat. Period. End of story. There is, by subtle implication, no further need for discussion.

What bothers the paleontologists is the certitude with which the geneticists assert when things took place. The genes most often used in such studies are not the genes that come down from both the father and the mother. Instead geneticists study the DNA found in tiny cells within the body cells—little organs called mitochondria. These little blobs of protoplasm provide the energy engine for each bodily cell and, importantly, they are passed down from generation to generation only by females. There is no sexual mixing of mitochondrial DNA. The only changes in it are what might be thought of as passive, resulting from such forces as natural background radiation. No one argues much about this, but suspicion arises when the natural changes over time in mitochondrial DNA (familiarly called mtDNA) are taken to be a precise calendar of events. On average, such changes (called mutations) are said to accumulate at a specific and usually very slow rate, knowledge of which comes from various estimates of time based on the evolutionary distance of one species from a related species. Evidently thousands of years can go by without a mitochondrial mutation. So this molecular clock is based, in other words, upon guesses that may be true, on average, or may not. Such guesses probably have a great deal more likelihood of being accurate when the time period measured by the calendar of mtDNA is in the millions of years. How such a tiny interval of time as 10,000 years is to be accurately reckoned is a bit obscure and is at best more of an art than a science.

On the other hand, paleontologists specify the timing of such matters by the most rigorous methods: radioactive decay—in the case of material from the last 50,000 years ago or less, by the known rate of decay of one form of carbon into another. This is called radiocarbon dating, and it can be accurate to within a couple of hundred years. But the paleontologist, like the archaeologist, requires the evidence provided by a carbon-containing specimen—such as a piece of wood or, in our concern here, the jawbone of a cat. And the main problem that paleontologists have with the origins of the domestic cat is that no certain remains of one have been found in the Near East and none are represented in drawings or etchings or other forms of Near Eastern art and craft in the period in question. Paleontologists tend to be pretty skeptical about anything that isn't represented by some form of physical evidence—fossils, bones, and preserved artifacts of nature like pollen, or illustrated on an ancient piece of bone or pottery.

The time and place of cat domestication therefore remains a subject that scientists can argue about, but no scientist is about to suggest that domestic cats did not arise originally from

the Near Eastern (née African) wild cat. The coat of the African version of the wild cat varies from reddish to sandy brown with thin broken stripes. The European version is more like the common tabby cat with a stronger pattern of stripes on a gray-brown coat. Speculation once was that while the African or (among geneticists) Near Eastern version led directly and first to the domestic cat, thereafter some European genes slipped in there to produce the domestic tabby (a word that refers to a pattern, not color). There are orange tabbies, as well as brown ones, and black ones where the coat and the stripes are almost the same color black. If indeed there were such a mixing, it was so minor as to be invisible to the molecular biologists. On the other hand, we do know that the tiniest change in a gene or set of genes can have considerable effect.

Whatever slight genetic changes occurred in the domestic cat aborning, it became smaller, with shorter legs and a smaller head—standard for most domesticated animals. Probably some slight alteration in gene expression powered by shifts in hormonal guidance led to the differences, though they were less pronounced than the changes accompanying the wolf's transition to dog.

The process did provide the domestic cat's coat with the opportunity to be multifariously colored and patterned. Most domestic cats throughout the world are tabbies, with blotchy coats with stripes and spots. (The word "tabby," by the way, comes from an Arabic word *Attabiya*, the name of a neighborhood in Old Baghdad where, according to Muriel Beadle, striped taffeta was manufactured.) Those tabbies that are mostly gray are called agouti, after a South American rodent whose coat is similar, its guard (outer) hairs banded in at least two colors. Two types of tabby patterns exist in domestic cats: (l) on which wavy vertical stripes run from the shoulder to the start of the tail, with those on the thighs tending to break up into spots, and (2) on which the stripes on the side of the body are horizontal, forming spiral-like patterns. In terms of variety in visible features including the coat, the differences between the official breeds of cat appear to be only a bit more various than the differences within a single breed of dog such as the Australian shepherd.

Nor did the changes wrought render the domestic cat almost wholly dependent upon humans as are most domesticates. Practically any house cat, to this day, can wander forth and make a pretty satisfactory living either as a feral neighborhood cat with the occasional handout, or as a lone hunter in the wild. Thus the domestic cat is not so much a true domesticate, one might say, as it is what Juliet Clutton-Brock, a zoologist at London's Natural History Museum, categorizes as an "exploited captive," a group that includes reindeer, yaks, camels, and llamas along with cats. By this, she means those animals "that have been made more tractable or tame but whose breeding does not necessarily involve intentional selection." Why, she suggests, would you mess around with the genes of a camel if you just want stuff and people carried across deserts? The animal is perfect for the purpose (although camels can be pretty nasty to people and a little more work on their disposition might well be in order).

Clutton-Brock is not wholly comfortable putting cats in the same category as yaks or camels, or with true domesticates like dogs. They really fit in both categories, she says, and might better be called "exploiting captives." This reminds one of the belief, held by most cat scholars now who look into cat domesti-

cation, that the cats took the main initiative, tamer ones producing ever tamer ones as they patrolled the granaries for rodents
and came ever closer to the humans.

In any event, Egyptian representations of cats have been
dated as far back as 2600 B.P.E. (Before Present Era, which is
the same as B.C. but less parochially theological). These might
well have been nondomesticated cats, as were (most likely) the
similar remains from about 9000 B.P.E. from Cyprus. A cache
of bones of seventeen cats and some little milk bowls, however,
were found in an Egyptian tomb dated to 1900 B.P.E. and they
seem more likely to be domestic cats. Why did it take so long to
get around to domesticating cats? The tomb with the bones and
bowls was in the middle of what is called the Middle Kingdom,
a thousand or so years after the first Egyptian dynasties. Surely
the wild cat had been hanging around permanent human habitations for as long as wolves had, starting about 14,000 B.P.E.
or earlier. There is no answer to why Egyptians took so long to
domesticate the cat—or, if you please, for the cat to domesticate
itself.

But even if some other people—Babylonians or whoever—
actually (or also) domesticated the cat, there's no physical evidence that they or anyone else around this part of the world did
so. We can still say that the Egyptians may really deserve the
honor because once they found they had the domesticated cat
in their midst, they made a truly big deal of it. There are plenty
of Egyptian illustrations of cats sitting under the table or generally hanging around the way cats do, and sculptors had a field
day with them.

The Middle Kingdom Egyptians were great animal fanciers,
many of their deities being represented by wild animals, such

as Thoth, the god of writing, who appeared as a man with the head of an ibis. Anubis, who led dead people after death to the underworld and possible resurrection, is portrayed as a man with the head of a dog or jackal. Other deified creatures were the ram, the hawk, the baboon, the hippo, the crocodile, the frog, and the scarab beetle.

BASTET

In the long-lasting and shifting complexities of the great Egyptian kingdoms of prehistory, gods and goddesses came and went, morphing into new ones or combining with old ones, while ceremonial and political centers shifted from one place or another, such as Thebes or Memphis. By 2000 B.P.E., the two daughters of Ra the Sun God, a major deity among major deities, were represented as women with the heads of lionesses, bespeaking a fierce protectiveness of the sun, the pharaohs, and the Egyptian political and cultural order. One daughter was the goddess Bast, sometimes called Bastet, who later came to be shown as a woman with the head of a domestic cat, and took on the job of patron of fertility and pregnancy, a champion of women in general and of marriage.

CAT (THE SUN) AND THE SERPENT (DARKNESS). CAT APPEARS TO BE A SERVAL.

The cat, also sacred to the goddess Isis, was considered a protector as well as a rodent hunter, its talents including killing cobras (also known as asps). In fact, one famous illustration on papyrus shows a cat severing the head of a large serpent with a knife— perhaps representing the light ridding the world of darkness, or Ra

himself setting the night to flight—though the cat in question, with its spots and long ears, looks more like a serval than a house cat. Some scholars have suggested that the domestication of cats may have been hastened by putting tamed (and sacred) wild cats in temples and keeping them isolated there.

No one can doubt, however, that the Egyptians took their cats seriously. An inscription found at the royal tombs of Thebes reads as follows:

> Thou art the Great Cat, the avenger of the gods, and the judge of words, and the president of the sovereign chiefs and the governor of the holy Circle; thou art indeed . . . the Great Cat.

There are those who like to say that the cat has never forgotten how devoutly worshipped it once was.

In the meantime, some historians of catdom have argued that the Babylonians were the ones who pinned a bad rap on *black* cats, which have always been suspect in the hearts of humankind, likening them (when curled up sleeping) to coiled serpents. This favors the geneticists' view that cats were domesticated in the Near East earlier than the Egyptians are credited with. Or it may be wrong altogether: after all, seeing the shape of a snake in a cat seems a bit of a stretch, even a bit paranoid.

In any case, Bastet the cat goddess dwelled in a Nile delta city called Bubastis, and Herodotus has written that her temple, with its cats, was the most beautiful in all of Egypt. Annually up to 700,000 Egyptians made a raucous pilgrimage by boat along the delta waterways, women lifting their robes up over their heads and shouting ribald comments to those watching from the banks. At Bubastis a grand and evidently promiscuous celebration of Bastet and of cats and all they stood for took place during which, Herodotus reported, more wine was consumed in a few days than throughout the rest of the entire year, and there was a great deal of what the historian called "mischief."

Cats were also associated with the moon for a host of reasons. Like the moon, cats are nocturnal. And in the dark, their eyes glowed as if lit by the moon. Also, the pupils of their eyes could wax and wane much like the moon does over the month. The lunar connection, of course, associated cats with the lunar cycle of menstruation, which began a physico-spiritual liaison between women and cats that persists in some quarters to this day.

Throughout Egypt in those early times, uncounted households kept house cats, which were so highly regarded that when one aged and died, the entire family had to shave off their eyebrows in mourning. Killing a cat was considered a capital crime. Once a household cat died, it was mummified with the same care that dear relatives were, many of the cats being taken to Bastet's city to be buried in a huge cat necropolis. There were other ceremonial cat graveyards in other parts of the land as well.*

Once the cat cult or whatever it was truly caught on, it became de rigueur to sacrifice cats to Bastet, and huge catteries arose, producing young cats for sacrifice to the goddess, a case of religious devotion getting out of hand, as so often happens.

---

* According to Stephen Buckley of the University of York in England, the embalming substance for cats contained 80 percent fats or oil, 10 percent conifer resin, 10 percent pistacia resin, and, wondrously, a pinch of cinnamon. Pistacia, by the way, is a flowering shrub, a member of the cashew family from which mastic is produced and which modern science has found—as did the ancient Egyptian mummifiers—to have antibacterial properties.

What had been a felony was now an act of piety. At this time, the Egyptians also had created the world's first puppy mills, providing other pilgrims with young dogs to sacrifice to the dog-headed Anubis.

Wherever cats indeed first became domesticated, they probably began their nearly worldwide fame in pagan Egypt as greatly esteemed creatures, symbols of highly desirable features of life and spiritual connection. After their domestication in Egypt, they were considered so important that if an Egyptian traveler found one in another kingdom, he would take it home with him to Egypt. Even with such care, however, cats made themselves comfortable on ships and other modes of trade travel and spread around the Mediterranean and thence to the rest of the inhabited world. But while they were esteemed in Egypt, in other parts of the world, and notably in Christian Europe, their reputation would take a sorry turn for the worse.

Black cat observes the making of magic as a Kwakiutl carver produces a totem pole in Alert Bay, British Columbia.

Chapter 3
Black Cats and Feline Reputations

Beware of people who dislike cats.

—IRISH PROVERB

ost people in the United States have heard that if a black cat crosses your path, bad luck will follow. Most people who respond to such an event by saying something like "uh-oh" don't follow up and blame the cat for the fact that a few days later they are, say, fired from their job or trip over the dog and sprain an ankle. But the notion persists, as do many other folk beliefs about cats-as-trouble. Most of these notions arose (in the West) during the late Middle Ages, persisting well into the seventeenth and even the eighteenth centuries. They come down to us today, happily, for the most part filtered by time and reason into paler, less scary versions. In fact, in England it is good luck if a black cat crosses your path. But Europeans in earlier times found plenty of reasons to be truly horrible to cats, especially black ones.

Black cats were not only nocturnal like all cats, skulking around in the dark as if guilty of something, and they were

often indifferent to humans, even haughty, but also they had
the misfortune of being black. For Europeans in early times,
black was—simply—bad. It was associated with the underworld, with night (when bad things like werewolves were on the
prowl), with the dark forests where dangerous spirits and crazy
people bent on mayhem lurked. It was a scary world, where
Satan himself was a constant threat. He and his dark minions
practiced the black arts and were always looking to traduce innocent souls into evil.* The world, back in late medieval times,
was also full of somewhat attenuated beliefs based on ancient
times. Rome's Diana the Huntress was associated with cats and
later in her career morphed a little bit into Hecate, goddess of
the underworld and given to dark doings. Also she was associated with the moon, that unreliable and protean body in the
night sky. Cats were awarded these attributes.

Early on, the Catholic Church tried to dispel any such pagan
notions, discouraging belief in the witchcraft that appears to
have always been part of life in most preliterate societies. But
late in the Middle Ages when universal satisfaction with the
teachings and workings of the Church began to decay, scape-
goats were needed. In 1233, Pope Gregory IX explained that
black cats were satanic and suddenly the Christian world was
overrun with witches and their "familiars," which is to say the
black cats that the witches sent forth to do harm to people.
Indeed, witches often turned into black cats. And witches of
course were agents of the devil. Thousands of people, mostly
women, were burned at the stake along with their cats. Putative

* It is an interesting sidelight that Samuel Vaughan, one of the great editors
of late-twentieth-century book publishing, claimed that the two most overused
words in American writing were "dark" and "light."

witches were typically tortured, and they readily admitted their guilt to stop the torture, even repeating various totally made-up incantations. Thus the virulence of witchcraft was proved, leading to a kind of mass hysteria in which yet more witches were put to the torch. Meanwhile, with such a bad rap, cats of all colors were persecuted.

In one common event, they were hung in bags that avid medieval sportsmen would attack with lances. Indeed, killing cats by one means or another was a highly popular pastime. In these exercises, there was no special emphasis on black cats—any cat would do. From this era comes the old saying "no room to swing a cat," another sportsmen's amusement. Possibly harking back to the Egyptian belief that cats were associated with fecundity, some medieval European farmers would bury a cat—alive—near each field they planted, to ensure the growth of the crops. In one macabre case, English archaeologists in the nineteenth century found the remains of thousands of cats buried by the adoring ancient Egyptians, and shipped them back to Albion to be ground up and used as fertilizer.

Mistreatment of cats in this era took many forms. As James Serpell of the University of Pennsylvania describes it,

> On feast days as a symbolic means of driving out the Devil, cats, especially black ones, were captured, tortured, thrown onto bonfires, set alight and chased through the streets, impaled on spits and roasted alive, burned at the stake, plunged into boiling water, whipped to death, and hurled from the tops of tall buildings; and all, it seems, in an atmosphere of extreme festive merriment.

Europe was not alone in the world in its distaste for all that cats stood for. Evil cats were common features of some Oriental folklore. In Japan, huge vampire cats took the form of human females and sucked the blood and strength from unwitting men. The Japanese used to cut off cats' tails, believing the tail to be the seat of their malevolence. On the other hand, cats were looked upon with great favor in many Japanese monasteries, where bobtail cats called temple cats or kimono cats were thought to exemplify much of the wisdom passed on by the Buddha. And today, the Japanese have given the world the *manekineko* or beckoning cat, which can be found in many Asian restaurants and homes in this country as well as Japan and the rest of Asia. The ceramic figure, something like a children's illustration, recalls a

MANEKINEKO

cat that legendarily stood at the entrance of a famous temple beckoning a feudal lord to come inside. A lightning bolt struck where the lord had been standing and thereafter the beckoning cat was taken to be an incarnation of the goddess of mercy. It is also said to be good for businesses, beckoning customers, and for happiness and harmony—a long way from the cat vampires of old.

Today in the West the association of cats with witches is memorialized in Hallowe'en costumery and iconography wherein witches on broomsticks ride across the disc of the full moon, while cartoonish black cats with malevolently arched backs spit and hiss in the foreground. On the last day of October, diminutive witches with black pointy hats will now turn up on doorsteps cheerfully calling for tricks or treats. And, of course, at least 278 zillion people have read about Harry Potter whose witch-filled world is also populated by kneazles, catlike creatures with spots and big ears, that appear to be mostly benevolent. In Islamic countries, cats are and were much admired, especially since the prophet Mohammed was particularly fond—and respectful—of cats, once cutting off his sleeve rather than awakening the cat who was sleeping on it. On the other hand, most Muslims find dogs objectionable. Dogs are eaten in many Asian restaurants, but I know of no place where cats are part of the normal diet.

The idea that a black cat crossing your path is bad luck is a southern European and Irish superstition, exported to the Americas. The English, as noted earlier, consider such an event good luck, and here and there local superstitions suggest that the appearance of a black cat in the presence of a pregnant woman assures a healthy offspring. Cats, and especially black ones, seem to have enjoyed a remarkable power: to be (in one place or another or at one time or another) all things to all people. Even at the height of cat persecution, plenty of cats lived comfortably with families who valued them for their help in vermin control. Indeed, in some places in England, if someone killed your cat, he would be forced to provide you with a pile of grain as high as the cat was long.

I myself had a black cat for several years. I did not seek him out. Instead, two women in the office where I worked at the time thought it would be funny (I suppose) or somehow fitting for them to present me with a large carton at the end of one October day—it was a few days before Hallowe'en—in which there sat a lanky young black cat with a look in his eyes of what seemed low-level outrage. The carton itself was decorated with various kinds of feline graffiti. I was unable to think of a graceful, or even ungraceful, way to refuse this gift, but the thought of schlepping the elaborately decorated carton to Grand Central Terminal in New York City and boarding a crowded train for the

hour's ride to my town, then arriving at my door and trying to explain to my then wife how we had come to have a cat and then introducing the cat to our dog while our three young daughters enthusiastically mauled it . . . well, it was not an auspicious beginning.

I was aware that black cats had a reputation for bringing bad luck, but as a science editor I was not going to worry about such nonsense. We found it difficult for reasons I don't recall to come up with a name for this interloper, so finally, in a burst of paternal authority (this was the late 1960s) and stunning imagination I unilaterally named him Cat. Science or no, I was tempted to look up a few superstitions about black cats and found, of course, that I should be careful about him crossing my path, and if he did the antidote was something like walking around the point where I had seen him twelve times, then heading off backwards in my original direction. I pronounced myself grateful for my exposure to science, thinking how time-consuming it would be for me to feel I needed the antidote, what with Cat strolling though the house day in and day out. Imagine the superstitious life: you would have hardly any time for anything else.

Anyway, I came to know Cat and to be very fond of him, admiring all the things about cats that all cat people admire, though if he ever caught a mouse and dispatched it (or a bird, for that matter), I was unaware of it. I did not consider this a failing—just Cat's amiable and, I thought, admirable approach to life. He took things easy and stayed out of trouble. Like most people, I have experienced plenty of misfortunes, mostly minor ones, but it has never occurred to me to blame any of them on Cat, who was a really good guy. One day, in his late teens, without having shown much by way of signs of aging, he simply stopped being alive.

I have since learned that nowadays it is not always easy to obtain a black cat from an animal shelter in the days near Hallowe'en. This is because some of the good people who devote themselves to such places do not want to run the risk of someone taking a black cat off to some horrid altar and performing lethal satanic rituals with it. This, in the twenty-first century!

It is a sad commentary to think that such a precious and complicated organ as the human brain, capable of designing a laser, or a symphony, or a democratic constitution, or of divining the common molecular basis for all of life on this planet, can still be so foully and stupidly misused.

Not all superstitions about cats that persist today are malevolent, of course; most of them are positive and harmless, if a bit silly. Upon reflection, it does seem strange for an animal whose evolutionary history is so steadfastly catlike—you have to go back many millions of years to find a cat ancestor that doesn't look and act unmistakably like a cat—to be assigned so variegated an array of meanings. The human propensity to imagine the supernatural or the anthropocentric and pin it on perfectly innocent animals is astonishing. Snakes have, as noted, gotten an especially bad rap (aside from the fact that some are poisonous) for conning Eve, and other offenses. Most American Indian cultures believe the presence of an owl, and especially the hooting of an owl, presages a death. Who doesn't—deep down—believe that the bluebird brings happiness? Dogs have both suffered and been esteemed in their symbolic essences. Horses come off pretty well in this regard: malevolent horses are rarely seen in human folklore or in the tribunals of people of faith.

Cats and dogs are considered either contemptible or splendid in a kaleidoscope of ways and for a host of reasons. The Church of Rome, for example, found dogs to be despicable because of their licentiousness but also heroic for their loyalty. The Church held cats in some contempt (not only were they licentious but they were noisy about it) until a papal successor to Pope Gregory IX began raising them. Then attitudes toward cats slowly changed to mostly positive. Today, in the United States, more cats are pets than dogs.

We have been talking about cats as seen in the mirror that many people carry around, imagining that their own reflections project some truth about the rest of nature. These are what Michael Sims, the scholar of the remarkable tales of archy and mehitabel†, calls "symbolic delusions." It seems to me that all such notions—complimentary ones as well as utterly insulting ones, none of which has been solicited by cats themselves—are, if anything useful at all, a version of a Rorschach test, those ink blot examinations that humans use to try to figure out other humans. But this is a book about real cats, so the rest of it will

THE CHESHIRE
CAT

endeavor to tell the story of cats largely from their own point of view, as best we can perceive that.

†These tales were told by archy, a philosophical cockroach, who wrote by leaping at night upon letter after letter on the typewriter of a reporter, Don Marquis. But archy could not make capital letters or most punctuation marks. His friend mehitabel was a formerly aristocratic cat who had fallen on hard times but always kept her head high and her dreams optimistic.

PART TWO
CATWORK

The two essentials for any living animal are to eat and to

reproduce. So we look in on the ways of nature's

most efficient predators, and how they arrange their

lives to accomplish these requirements.

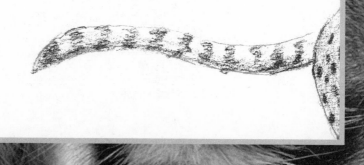

DAUGHTER SALLY'S NEW KITTEN, DELILAH, STALKS AND POUNCES.

Chapter 4
On Being a Predator

What immortal hand or eye
Could frame thy fearful symmetry
—*The Tiger,* BY WILLIAM BLAKE

othing in nature is perfect, it seems. Even the most superbly evolved predators on earth (meaning cats) have their limitations, limitations that can under certain evolutionary circumstances turn around and bite the near-perfect predator, leading to extinction. We saw this with the demise of the great saber-tooths, who evidently vanished when their *relatively* slow and oversized prey vanished from the scene. The cheetah's style—racing at full speed after a gazelle at some sixty miles an hour (some say seventy) and using their prominent dewclaws on the front legs to hook the gazelle and bring it down in a cloud of dust—seems highly efficient, but it isn't perfect. If such a chase is too prolonged (which many are), even if it succeeds in bringing down the gazelle, the cheetah may be so exhausted that, while she recovers, others like hyenas or leopards can steal in and snatch the cheetah's booty.

Being a cheetah, then, can be a risky business, and at one

time or another in its recent past (meaning a few thousand years ago), Africa's cheetah population suffered a huge and yet unexplained collapse, leaving a meager few to carry on. One result was a new population of cheetahs derived from so few founders that today's cheetahs are virtually identical genetically, which is to say severely inbred. Loss of genetic diversity can be dangerous, leading to reproductive and other physiological difficulties as well as a reduced genetic ability to respond adaptively to any major change in the environment (such as, perhaps, unusually prolonged drought from global warming). Getting mammals to breed in captivity puts a burden on their reproductive vitality—particularly a psychological burden. Among cheetahs captive breeding is extremely difficult and rare and until recently zoos bent on breeding captive populations of endangered species have been baffled by cheetahs. In fact, no one had successfully bred captive cheetahs since the reign in India in the fourteenth century of Akbar the Great until the Cincinnati Zoo managed it in the 1970s.

The predatory style of the cheetah, of course, is highly specialized and has virtually nothing in common with the style of the domestic cat and all the other feline and pantherine members of the family whose approach is typically a matter of stealth and relatively brief chases by lone hunters or, alternatively, waiting silently in ambush. Lions are an obvious exception to the single hunter mode. A cat hunt is almost the exact opposite of the likes of wild dogs and wolves, who are built for endurance running and hunt in packs. Wolf hunts are successful a surprisingly low number of times, one success out of some twenty attempts being fairly common. But canids can also include fruit and other vegetation in their diets. Cats are obligate carnivores:

they are obliged to eat meat almost exclusively, whether it is mouse meat or that of a huge water buffalo. The gut of cats is shorter than that of most dog types, because the digestion of meat can be accomplished in a smaller amount of space and time than vegetable matter. They also lack the flattened molars for grinding up vegetable matter that the canids have.

All the cats are digitigrade, meaning they walk and run on their toes. What we think of as their feet are in fact mostly toes, while the rest of the "foot" extends up to what we would think of as a knee but what is in fact their version of a wrist. These are evolutionary changes that facilitate high-speed running. In hoofed animals like deer and antelopes and horses, the hard claw of one toe became the hoof—a condition called unguli-grade, hoofed grazing animals being known in zoological circles as ungulates. Hoofs are also adaptations to the running life. On the other extreme are animals like bears and humans who are plantigrade, planting the entire foot down on the ground with each step. This makes for a slower pace than a digitigrade animal.

All the cats, including yours if you have one (and most of the dog species, too), are relatively long-legged com-pared with such animals as weasels or pandas or squirrels

How
CLAWS WORK

or mice—another adaptation to the running life, especially if the running is to take place on relatively open land. Local varia-tions can be seen even within a species—jaguars, for instance. Those jaguars that dwell in the close quarters of South and Cen-tral American forests tend to have shorter legs than those who live in more open territory.

We will look at other physical adaptations to the life of the predator in a later detailed chapter on the senses of cats. Suffice

it for now to say the cat has twelve separate muscles serving each radar antenna-like ear, and the cat's eyes work well in both day and night. Here we will observe some of the details of the predatory strategies cats (including domestic cats) use, of which there are two main types: mobile, where the cat actively seeks out prey; and stationary, where the cat waits silently for the action to come to him or her. It may be no surprise that there is a fair amount of misinformation—sometimes labeled myth—about the hunting behavior of cats, and this will be gently dispelled. For example, some cats, including some domestic ones, are scavengers. Indeed, biologists point out that the cat food we supply from the supermarket is not killed by the cat, so eating it is at least technically scavenging. Some biologists like making such distinctions.

What follows is an imaginary hunt by a domestic cat, based on a good deal of ethological observation by scientists over the years. It is not easy to observe a cat hunting, since the observer is likely to be apparent to the cat and therefore may cause it to change its behavior in one way or another, being a distraction at the very least. Hunting cats, for obvious reasons, tend to be secretive, and it is not every field biologist who has seen a lynx catch a snowshoe hare in the snows of Canada, or a cougar take down a mule deer in Rocky Mountain National Park. Ethology, the study of animal behavior in the wild, came in the latter half of the twentieth century to be a highly technical and complicated task, involving Herculean note taking and the patience of at least a demigod, all of this over a period not of hours or days but many months, even years. Jane Goodall spent more time observing chimpanzees than most anthropologists ever log with a given tribe of people, and more time than a lot of parents spend with their children.

In the hunt I'm about to describe (with thanks to the ethologists on whose shoulders I stand here), you may imagine your own cat as the hunter if you have one. Or you can, like me, imagine that the hunter is Cat, my old friend from decades ago, a sinewy, insinuating, and surreptitious character with glossy black fur and utterly expressionless, often unblinking yellow eyes. The tip of his tail switches back and forth whenever something in the environment moves, catches his ear or eye, and thereby arouses his interest.

It is early dusk in late May in the foothills of the Rocky Mountains. The sun has been down for some time, but the western sky is still light. Cat has finished his dinner of canned meat. Susanne doesn't feed him most commercially available dry cat foods, which contain vegetables, ever since she learned that vegetables are something no self-respecting wild cats eat. We have gone along with Cat's preferences as an obligate carnivore. Though comfortably full and without hunger, Cat heads off on the hunt. Why? Mainly because that is what cats do from time to time, whether they are hungry or not.

Thanks to drought conditions, I have not mowed the large backyard that is home to pasture grasses and various weeds like wild geranium and dandelions. Right now it is a bit overgrown, and a few birds—sparrowlike house finches with swatches of red on their heads—are looking for seeds on the ground under the tatterdemalion grass and weeds.

Cat sets his sights on one of the birds and in a low crouch he takes a few silent though quick steps toward the bird, then stops, staring, tail tip switching. Cat has some sense that he is on a fool's errand. Birds are especially hard to catch, what with vision that is nearly 360 degrees. The bird seems not to notice

him, however, so Cat moves closer, then even closer. Now only about ten yards separate the two.

Then from high in a cottonwood tree on the edge of the backyard, another house finch *chirts* in irritation. The house finches in the grass all stop and look around. The jig is up, Cat knows. He's been spotted by the finch in the tree. The bird's alarm call is really an emotional response to the irritation it feels on seeing the stalking cat, and not probably the deliberate and altruistic work of a guard on duty. In any event, the finches on the ground have been alerted. Cat is now on the radar of the birds on the ground and he knows that if he moves any closer, they will leave. Capable of flying off in any direction—their world is more a three-dimensional place than Cat's world—the birds will not be caught this night.

So Cat moves on, trotting off in another direction to the cattle gate and into the pasture beyond, where the grass grows higher and one can hunt without being seen. Along the way, he stops from time to time, looking up and around.

Being a male, and not having any obligations such as bringing food home to kittens, Cat would far prefer to find a young rabbit to pounce on, but he is in competition for rabbits with the coyotes (who would also like to catch Cat). The coyotes have run the rabbits off this year, so it is field mice or voles tonight. He could hunt down a vole, but he usually doesn't since they, being insectivores, do not taste very good. And, happily, Cat can smell the mouse urine that marks the trails mice take through the tall grass, and he knows just where one such trail leads. Within minutes he is a few feet from a mouse burrow. He drops down low to the ground behind a large clump of grass, and keeps his ears peeled for the sound of mice exiting the burrow, almost quiveringly ready to push off with his rear legs and pounce. He waits, immobile, eyes fixed in the direction of the unseen mouth of the burrow.

He waits. Minutes pass. He continues to wait, utterly motionless, listening.

And finally, after a few more minutes, he gives up on this burrow and trots off to a farther pasture. There he locates another burrow ("an interest in locus" in science-speak) and waits a few feet away from it in the tall grass, staring from yellow eyes, the black pupils large in the gathering dusk. He listens to the high-pitched voices of mice and presently he hears the scratching of small feet in the dirt. Every cell of his body seems focused on the mouth of the burrow. The sound of the tiny feet changes as they go from dirt to grass. Cat springs, pounces, and seeing now the furry juncture of head and body, he clamps down, eyeteeth sinking in, severing the mouse's vertebral column at the neck. The mouse instantaneously goes limp, dead.

Cat is suddenly afflicted by a sense of confusion. What should he do with the mouse? He bats it with a front paw and it flops over. Cat is not hungry. He has no urge to eat the mouse. But there it is. Caught.

He picks it up by the scruff of its broken neck and begins to trot back to the house through the tall grass and into the unmowed yard to the back door. He pays no attention to the alarm *chirts* of the house finches. He pushes through the dog door into the house, and sets the mouse down on the tiled floor near the clothes dryer. The urge to hunt has been fulsomely assuaged. Cat pads into the living room where he rubs himself against Susanne's ankle, purring, at ease.

One of the myths about cats is that once they settle in at a burrow to wait for some action, they may stay there motionless for hours on end. No close observations are known to confirm this; rather, cats (not being stupid) move on after a relatively short wait at an unproductive site. Another myth is that cats do not kill more than they can usefully consume, unless it is a situation like a bigger cat getting into the enclosed space of a chicken coop and leaving all the chickens dead. But as Cat just demonstrated in our imaginary hunt, the urge to go forth and snatch up a prey animal is not inevitably and always linked to hunger. It is a separate urge altogether, it seems, though the resulting behavior often winds up being the sequence of hunt, kill, eat.

Cats also have the option of caching their prey and coming back to eat at some later time. They are not necessarily averse to spoiled meat. This of course raises the idle question of whether eating cached meat that one killed the day before is just delayed ingestion or a kind of scavenging. The answer—probably—is simply that the categories with which we address the world of nature are often either imprecise or too precise.

Caching prey for later is apparently common among wild cats, including mountain lions. Some local friends of ours were walking their dogs in a large tract of Colorado Open Space near here when they realized that a mountain lion was crouching a few feet behind them. The lion began to hiss and scream, the dogs barked, the two women picked up branches to wield at the lion. The lion batted the branches away and continued the threat. One of the dogs, a golden retriever puppy, kept snapping at the lion's tail, eventually annoying the lion enough that it leapt into a tree. This allowed the women and their dogs to back away from the scene and escape to safety. Later, authorities said the lion was probably protecting a cache of food, and gave the women a ticket for being off the approved path, while the retriever puppy was named the state of Colorado hero of the month by the governor's office—all of this suggesting that matters of justice in lion–human relations could use a little clarification. I know, I know. I grumbled about this before. You would too, most likely, if you had this most excellent predator in your front yard.

When do domestic cats hunt? Most people think of cats as particularly active at dusk or even at night, though in fact cats have peaks of activity during the day, unlike their African wild cat progenitors who are evidently altogether nocturnal. Domestic cats have apparently adapted themselves to the daily rhythms of the humans with whom they live, and many of them appear to be most comfortable sleeping through the night curled up on a human's bed or athwart the sleeping human's legs. (Feral cats whose lives are in very few ways dictated by human schedules tend to be active mostly at night. We will look into the world of the feral cat in later chapters.)

Observations suggest that virtually any well-fed household cat remains an effective hunter, meaning that you can relieve the cat's hunger yourself, but you can't take the predator out of the cat. Nor is it true, as some cat owners think, that if they feed their cats very sparingly they will be more avid hunters. It just risks making them unhealthy.

In all known cases, house cats (and most other cats) are lone hunters who take care not to hunt in proximity to other cats whose presence in the area is announced by marking hunting territory with urine signposts.

Cats generally pursue the prey animals you would expect.

One surprise is that most cats appear to be scared of adult rats, particularly the Norway rats that can be the scourge of urban places. They may help to control rat populations by preying on less-than-half-grown rats, but, overall, a cat is no solution to a serious rat infestation.

Another and highly effective way cats rid a place of mice and rats is the passive way—by their smell and that of the urine they spray around. This has been shown quite decisively by the Los Angeles Police Department, who began in 2001 to import cats from feral colonies onto the premises of different precinct headquarters. The mice and rats that had plagued the places were soon gone. It took about a month of caging the cats in their new homes for them to acclimatize to them (and not race back to their previous homes), and thereafter the cops had to feed the cats. But the vermin were gone—of course, to some other place in Los Angeles, but that was not the LAPD's problem.

The largest prey domestic cats will hunt are adult rabbits and hares, and relatively large birds like pheasants or ducks. Such large prey are harder to bring down, based on field observations of the number of pounces a cat makes before achieving success. In fact, it seems that it is chiefly male cats who are most likely to go after such large prey animals—not only because males tend to be bigger but also because they have no obligation, as females often do, to bring morsels back to waiting kittens. Catching an adult rabbit may take twice as long, but it weighs five times as much as a rodent like a vole, so one gets what amounts to more bang for the buck if, like males, one has the time—which mothering cats don't. It is faster and more efficient for females to catch mice or other small mammals (fewer pounces per kill), and evidence suggests that females—especially mother cats—

tend to be more skilled hunters than males, making optimum use of their time.

Some observers point out that cats will typically go after those prey animals that their mothers brought back to them when they were kittens in the nest. Another factor in prey choice is, of course, availability. One study showed that in autumn when rodents were at their yearly peak, it took cats an average of forty minutes to catch one. In early summer when rodents are at their seasonal low, it takes an average of seventy minutes for hunting to succeed.

Cats also prey on birds, leading to a nationwide controversy between cat lovers and bird lovers. (I happen to be both.) Mice and voles and wild hares have little in the way of legions of fans out to protect them, but bird lovers abound, especially lovers of songbirds and defenders of endangered species. An ornithologist friend of mine, Gene Morton, huffs that domestic cats are nothing but "subsidized predators." In North America, Europe, and elsewhere, birds show up in the contents of cats' stomachs or in their scat as some 20 percent of the total, and usually less than that, according to various estimates. One study showed that birds were only 8 percent of cats' prey, and of course any such study will vary from locale to locale. It seems that in most instances only a few bird species are taken regularly, mainly ground-feeding birds and especially starlings and house sparrows (along with pheasants). Sophisticated American bird lovers are not fond of starlings or house sparrows, both of them intrusive aliens who were unfortunately introduced to this continent and subsequently spread like weeds to the detriment of native songbird species. So, subsidized or not, we can give the cats at least two cheers for taking on the starling and house

sparrow invasion. (They have a long way to go; it is estimated that 600 million starlings live in North America, an almost unimaginably huge population explosion since some nitwit in New York City imported a bunch of them from Europe in the late nineteenth century.)

A recent study in England suggests that cats can reduce urban bird populations without actually killing them. It is claimed by scientists at the University of Sheffield that birds' fear of cat predation is enough to engender a failure to breed, or at least to reduce the usual number of chicks, thus bringing about a drop in overall bird numbers. Other scientists do not hold this study in much regard, saying that the computer model used is flawed and no one has ever demonstrated that birds show such a phenomena as a generalized fear.

The most devastating effect of feral cats arises from those on islands. Numerous species of birds and reptiles have been rendered extinct or steeply endangered on islands where wildlife previously lived without predators. For one example among the many, a large flightless parrot of New Zealand has been extinguished, chiefly by cats, except on a few nearby cat-free islands to which they have been exported as a conservation measure. In one bizarre case, on a small island near New Zealand, there lived a nearly flightless species of wren. In the late nineteenth century a lighthouse keeper arrived with a pet cat who, in one month, wiped out every one of the unique Stephen Island wren population by itself. Of course, it can get more complicated than that.

On Little Barrier Island off New Zealand, now a dedicated wildlife sanctuary, there is a small and endangered population of Cook's petrel, a seabird that lives in burrows and, because it evolved largely without predators, usually produces only one chick at a time. Scientists at the University of Aukland have been monitoring the petrel population over thirty-five years, noting that it was preyed upon by two main predators: small Pacific rats and feral cats, both of whom had been introduced to the island by humans more than a hundred years ago. The scientists measured the survivability of petrel chicks when both rats and cats were present: only one out of three chicks born survived, on average. The feral cats were removed from the island, but the expected increase in petrel survivability failed to materialize. Quite the contrary. With only rats left on the island to prey on the petrels, their survivability plummeted to a shocking one out of ten.

It seems that the cats were preying heavily on rats while snatching the occasional petrel, so the cats were in fact providing what might be thought of as a helpful service, based on the old adage that the enemy of my enemy is my friend. On the other hand, it was pretty clear that for the permanent safety of the petrels, the best idea was to rid the island of both alien predators, and once this was done, petrel survivability rose to three out of five. In any event, it all suggests that re-creating an ecosystem is more complicated than it might at first seem.

House cats, on their regular or irregular forays, probably do not account for much in the way of devastating bird losses. But colonies of feral cats can be a considerable drain on local bird populations and in such situations, rancorous arguments can and do break out between cat fanciers and bird lovers. One of the most noticeable such arguments arose in 2007 when a Galveston, Texas, bird expert shot a feral cat belonging to a colony that threatened the existence of the few remaining local members

of an endangered shorebird species, the piping plover, which nests and sleeps on the beach. The feral cat colony nearby was supported largely by a single individual who fed them daily. A lawsuit followed in which the cat feeder claimed ownership of the feral cats since he fed them and so they were, in effect, his pets—and therefore it was not legal to shoot any of them. The bird expert claimed he was acting in the spirit of federal laws to do with the protected status of endangered species and migratory birds. Faced with a choice between such difficult-to-reconcile viewpoints, the jury split down the middle and the case was dropped. And, of course, no light arose from all the heat.

Better ways of handling such situations can surely be invented than warring vigilantes taking shots at each other and taking each other to court. Before one gets involved in these matters (particularly in a hostile exchange), it is wise to look at the laws and traditions involved. For example, it seems that a person who claims ownership of a feral cat colony should provide a bit more than occasional, or even daily, food. Feral cats are typically stricken with parasites and diseases, many of which are dangerous not only to cats and wildlife but humans as well. Proper owners of cats look after these veterinary matters as a matter of course, along with taking a lot of other responsibilities for their feline wards. Feral cats are, if you think about it, not interested in being anyone else's property.

A legal difficulty that can be and has been invoked in such matters also is that if you are in fact the owner of a cat colony that preys freely on members of endangered or otherwise protected species of birds, you may be subject to fines and worse under the federal laws mentioned earlier. An increasingly vocal champion of the feline side of this complex debate is Alley Cat Allies, a national organization that represents the rights of feral cats and seeks to educate the country on the need for a different animal-control system. In particular, the group advocates the use of trap-neuter-return, which is relatively self-explanatory, rather than a continuing slaughter of cats who, it points out, promptly replace themselves at any locale where they have been exterminated. Better to allow a handful of neutered adults to remain. Of course, the bird proponents then point out that neutered adult cats returned to the scene are still skilled predators of birds.

There is no simple answer. Enormous numbers of people love cats, feral or not, and are not about to put up with violence and mayhem directed at them. The bird-watching industry in the United States is a multibillion-dollar affair; to these many millions of loyalists can be added the legions of people who own pet birds. As a purely political science–type of observation, my guess is that the bird people can marshal much greater political power than the feral cat enthusiasts, who are far fewer and far less organized nationally. Given that, plus the laws of the land, I suspect that the bird people will prevail at least legally, especially (and not unreasonably) in those situations where endangered species are concerned. If there is one thing about feral cats that neither side can avoid admitting, it is that feral cats are not an endangered species. Estimates of the number of feral cats in the United States range between fifty and ninety million, and it is highly unlikely that there will be enough feral cat fanciers to protect very many of them. Of course, climate change is slated to mess up the already disappearing habitat and migratory routes of many bird species (the chief reasons for their decrease nowadays are land development and power lines, followed way down the line by feral cats). North America is likely to lose as much as a third of its more than eight hundred bird species to oblivion within the next century. Feral cats, on the other hand, may well outlast us all, compact little leopards numbering in the tens of millions, patrolling the landscape day and night.

If indeed, as paleontologist Alan Turner says, a domestic cat is anatomically a scaled-down version of a leopard, then how do domestic cats stack up against their more charismatic cousins as predators? In sheer speed, the domestic cat is no match for its larger relatives. A domestic cat is capable of speeds up to thirty miles an hour. Cheetahs may be capable of seventy miles an hour in short bursts, fast enough to catch a Thomson's gazelle that can reach sixty miles per hour, which in turn is ten miles an hour faster than a lion can go in relatively short bursts.

Most cats, big and small, stalk prey in much the same manner, keeping low to the ground, pausing to watch, whiskers spread and ears facing forward, then darting forward in the attempt to catch the prey. (In bird hunting, they don't always pause and stalk, but also run at the bird in hopes of catching it in their paws before it flies off.) When predator meets prey, the smaller cats typically grab the small mammal with their teeth, but the large cats will hold larger prey with one or two paws and bite its throat just in front of the paw-hold, allowing the predator to readjust the killing bite as needed or to shove the prey off balance. Among all the carnivores—bears, wolves, and so forth—cats are the only ones to use their paws this way.

Like Cat in our imaginary hunt, most of the smaller wild cats take their prey in a bite to the nape of the neck, severing the spinal cord. The large cats, on the other hand, typically taking larger prey—and sometimes prey larger than themselves—go for a bite to the throat that cuts off the windpipe and smothers the prey, or put their mouths over the mouth and nose of the prey, also leading to suffocation. In larger prey, the neck is simply too broad for a nape bite to work. Smaller cats, including domestic ones, crouch over their prey to feed on it, while the big cats will typically lie down and hold the prey in their paws, once they have looked around to assure themselves that no other predators or scavengers are threatening their catch. Hiding food, setting it aside in caches, is common among all the wild cats, and only cheetahs rarely if ever scavenge because, it is suspected, their efficiency in the hunt is so great as to render scavenging unnecessary. Leopards are, of course, famous for hauling their prey up into a tree, which thwarts even gathering vultures.

Lions break the mold of the lone hunter, associating in groups called prides that typically consist of several related females and a male or two. The usual story of lion hunting tells of an astoundingly complex, well-coordinated group effort. Lions do sometimes drive prey into the clutches of others waiting in ambush (as do lynxes sometimes as well). But this kind of hunt is evidently rare. George Schaller, one of the greatest big-cat watchers of all time, found that the optimal size of a group of hunting lions, in terms of hunting efficiency, is *two*. Any more than that and food intake per lion was reduced. Indeed, it has been suggested that lions associate in groups for reasons other than hunting, a topic that will be explored in a later chapter on cat society. It could be that lions live in groups so that some of them can scavenge off the hunters in the pride, especially in times of plenty. Since the pride is made up of kin, this is better (from the standpoint of spreading one's genes) than letting strange, unrelated lions—or, worse, hyenas and jackals—scavenge. In any case, it seems that large prides of lions support a certain number of slackers, especially males.

DC's territory includes a bureau drawer in his Tucson home.

Chapter 5

Homeland Security

. . . when the moon gets up and the night comes, he is the Cat that walks by himself, and all places are alike to him.

—RUDYARD KIPLING

Not quite. Most cats are intensely territorial, no matter how often or far they go on nightly forays, and if "the Cat that walks by himself" strays into the homeland of another male, he may well get his head handed to him. The writer Wright Morris had it closer to reality when he wrote, "Cats don't belong to people. They belong to places." Some people will tell you that if you move, leave the cat behind because he's going to find his way back there one way or another. Others say that you should let the cat be first in a new residence so he can establish his new territory without interference. These are all old wives' tales (or urban myths or whatever is okay to say these days), but they do bespeak the nearly universal interest of cats in their own places.

Of course, Kipling had it mostly right when he called the cat a loner: most are. Yet exceptions to that exist—as to virtually everything in the world. Lions and some feral cats are highly social (for cats, anyway). Male cheetahs tend to hang out with

one another; no one knows why. But most cats—both wild and domesticated—have a homeland that they defend against encroachment by other cats, especially cats of the same sex. On the other hand, in some cases, particularly in the case of females, territories can overlap a little without causing hostilities.

All of which is to say that very little about the preferences of cats is cut-and-dried. Even so, expert cat watchers have discerned general patterns in the kind of space cats put between each other and to what end they do this.

To begin with, untold numbers of domestic cats live in home ranges that are proscribed by the walls of an urban apartment, their territories thus being matters largely outside feline control. Scientists interested in the territoriality of cats rarely study such situations. To be sure, many cats seem perfectly content to live their lives entirely indoors in what might strike a wild or feral cat as far too limited a space. Such house-bound cats, however, enjoy on a regular basis one of the main determinants of the territorial size to which cats aspire, which is to say food. A sufficient food supply is the major determining factor for female cat territories, and an important factor for males. But male cats' territories are primarily based on what might be called a guy thing. They are on average some three to three and a half times the size of a female's territory, allowing the male to exert some degree of exclusive control over several females.

Tomcats are, of course, notoriously polygynous, and part of the excitement of cat life is multiple sex partners, an excitement most females indulge in as well despite the best efforts of the reigning male to keep other males at bay. On the other hand, sexual and reproductive behavior on the part of most cats who live entirely inside a house or apartment is severely restricted.

Even in multicat apartments, cats rarely bump into potential sexual partners, usually because such cats tend to have been neutered. They are thus of little interest to biologists seeking The True Nature of Cats, though of course they command the attention of veterinarians who devotedly look after the health of these feline equivalents of hothouse orchids.

Cats who can roam free—farm cats, suburban or country cats, and of course feral cats who will be discussed in some detail in a later chapter—establish home ranges that can be anywhere from two-tenths of an acre to as much as 420 acres, depending on how well fed they are. Females look for an area that not only provides sufficient prey to satisfy their own hunger and that of their kittens but also has at least one satisfactory den or other site for giving birth and nurturing the kittens.

When a cat (say a female cat) sets out from the barn or the house for her *home range*, she will usually follow a traditional path. Part of the path may lead to the home range of another cat, and is peaceably used on a first-come, first-served basis. Evidently, if both cats arrive at an intersection at the same time, they may sit still for a long period waiting for one to take the initiative and make the crossing. What instigates this first move is not known. Several paths may radiate from our female cat's home range—leading to places for resting, hunting, or defecation.

Her home range can be any shape, depending on circumstances (in the diagram it is round) and it has several inner ranges of decreasing size. First is the *ter-*

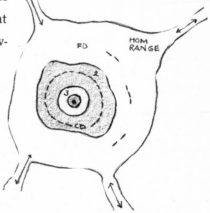

CAT SOCIAL DISTANCES:
↔   PATHS IN AND OUT
1   HOME RANGE
FD FLIGHT DISTANCE
2   TERRITORY
CD CRITICAL DISTANCE
3   SOCIAL DISTANCE
CAT SITS INSIDE PERSONAL
DISTANCE
(AFTER BEAVER)

ritory, the area the cat will defend against encroachment by feline strangers. Among domesticated cats, the territory is usually the same as the home range, but in wild cats it is smaller in extent than the home range. Within the territory is an area dubbed *social distance*; inside that is *personal distance*. Our female cat will have certain acquaintances (us, for example) whom she will let have intimate contact, even touching her, within her personal distance. Other lesser acquaintances will be reminded by threatening displays to stay farther off in the realm of social distance.

In addition, there is another invisible (to us) line called the *flight distance*. If a strange creature—for example, an unknown human or dog—crosses that line, the cat will flee.* If for some reason our female cat cannot flee, she will wait till the stranger reaches the *critical distance* where she will attack it. If the female cat has a litter of kittens, the critical distance will be farther than her intimate personal space. All of these distances vary from cat to cat.

Male cats have a similar array of ranges, but they tend to be more territorial than females (meaning quicker to fight an intruder), and have larger territories, as noted. On the other hand, their home ranges may not have anything like a fixed outer boundary; instead, they may roam far and wide until they run into another male or some other obstacle. At the same time, males will let females into their territories but not into their intimate personal space. All of these social distances—from territories to personal space—are of particular importance to loners like cats,

---

* Virtually every mammal has its flight distance. Modern zoos like the Smithsonian's National Zoological Park and many others have designed animal enclosures that keep visitors outside a given animal's flight distance, and this permits the animal on display to go about its business without anyone coming too close, thus reducing stress.

and apply pretty much across the board to all the wild cats as well. Male tigers, for example, have territories that include several female territories, which they defend often with lethal ferocity against other males. The subtle and to us often invisible spatial preferences of cats are an essential means by which cat society, as limited as it may seem, is regulated and perpetuated.

Most cats, says veterinarian Bonnie Beaver of Texas A&M University, "form a much stronger bond with home range and territory than with any social being." And this humbling pronouncement of course applies to doting human owners as well as to sex partners. A friend of mine, Sally, who lives in Boulder, Colorado, told me a tale of two cats that illustrates this point almost to the point of caricature. When she was a girl her family left Ann Arbor, Michigan, to spend a year in Puerto Rico, leaving her cat, Rackety Coon, in the care of a neighbor. Soon enough Rackety disappeared from the neighborhood. When Sally and her family returned, she took on a gimpy-legged cat who belonged to a professor who was leaving town for good. This cat, named Mamselle, immediately made herself at home. At this point Rackety Coon appeared and he was mad as hell at having his personal house invaded by an interloper. Rackety Coon had been lurking around, making do by himself, waiting for the family to return. But to Mamselle, Rackety was the interloper. The two cats eventually worked out a way of staying out of each other's way most of the time, but their paths inevitably would cross, leading to ferocious squalling and fighting. This went on for *eighteen years*, a remarkable example of the implacable territoriality of some cats, not to mention the patience of some humans.

For all their territorial instincts, untold numbers of cats wander off and get lost. Evidence has accumulated from the Humane Society and other rescue organizations that dogs who are lost are more likely to be found than cats. The reasons are not officially clear but more than likely it has to do with the fact that many domestic cats spend a great deal of time not in the presence of their owners. Therefore it takes a longer time for the cat owner to realize the cat is missing. And longer to call the Humane Society or the local pound to see if his or her cat has turned up. Why do cats get lost? Some of them are simply leaving the domestic life to fetch up in a feral colony. And of course cats are curious, sometimes leading to misadventure.

Another friend of mine, Jane Poynter, when she was a young girl in Sussex, England, had a cat who got lost. Evidently Tom Tom was exploring the brick wall of a deep well and fell in, winding up some twenty feet down in two or three feet of water. He alternately swam and tried to climb the sheer walls, getting nowhere and abrading his claws down to nothing. Finally, after about six hours, the family heard him calling out. (They could hardly be blamed for not looking in a well for a cat.) They lowered the bucket and somehow got Tom Tom to crawl into it, then cranked him up to dry land and safety.

While female cats look primarily for home ranges that supply them (and their kittens) with sufficient food, the primary goal of the male is to establish a home range that includes the maximum number of females. Contrast this with dogs, highly social animals who do not seem to have much in the way of personal or social distances even when it comes to total strangers. For cats, successful reproduction and thus the perpetuation of the species is very much a matter of spatial relations and a fine precision about boundaries.

On the other hand, cat sex tends to be raucous in execution and often chaotic in its promiscuity. The nocturnal snarling of tomcats competing for a female during a sexual melee in the back alley is a sound that can be all too familiar to city dwellers. Whatever is going on out there in the middle of the night, it is definitely not what anyone would call a tender moment of love. The immediate results of all this noise from our human point of view were aptly described by the French writer, Emile Zola, discussing his female cat:

> She would come home in a shocking state, all bedraggled, her fur so torn and dirty that she had to spend a whole week licking herself clean. After that she would resume her supercilious airs . . . And one fine morning she would be found with a litter of kittens.

It may come as a surprise that male cats tend to be a bit fussy about sex. They are not fussy about partners but about place. If a female in estrus turns up in an unfamiliar place the male has strayed into, he may have to spend several days just patrolling the place, shooting urine around, rubbing the glands on his face on things, all to make himself comfortable. Otherwise, he will simply not feel sufficiently at home to be able to mate with the female who, in the meantime, may well have gotten it on with more familiar males. The male with temporary erectile dysfunction, however, could still get to impregnate her; members of a single cat litter quite often have different fathers.

Marking territory makes all the difference. Male cats lay claim to an area by spraying urine backwards onto various vertical surfaces. In the wild, rocks, trees, and bushes all serve as posts for these messages. Male cat urine has a very strong smell,

and people with male cats in their houses become all too aware
of it when their male marks the sofa or the dining room table
by way of making himself at home. Neutering the male is the
only hope in this situation, and it often doesn't help. Our Persian Rudolph was neutered but took the occasion daily to spray
urine on the clothes dryer. Even more trying was that our teenagers would often snatch something from the dryer and leave
the door open, providing Rudolph with an even more interesting area to spray: the inside of the dryer. I have no idea why
Rudolph wanted other cats to know that he had been there.

Periodically a male cat will sally forth around the perimeters
of his home range and refresh these signposts, updating the
information thereon for any cat who might wander in. Such
marking does not seem to threaten other male cats, telling
them to stay away. Instead, other males may mark the same
spots, "covering" the home cat's signal. So the marking would
seem to be a way that cats simply keep track of who has visited
recently. Females do a lot less of this sort of thing, but when
estrus is imminent, they busy themselves marking their home
range and advertising the good news to males far and wide; it
says, essentially, to all and sundry, "Why don'tcha come up and
see me sometime?"

To be sure, the female cat is very much a vamp during and
just before estrus. Aristotle pointed out that female cats "are
very lascivious, and make advances to the male." Indeed, the
pre-estrus advertising serves to bring in several males, assuring
her a good mix of potential mates. And while what eventually
ensues often looks and sounds less than voluntary, the female
is very much in charge throughout. If she takes a dislike to a
given male, he doesn't have a prayer.

Caterwauling is a word created originally in German to denote the howls and screeching of a cat in heat, but it is not the female who is responsible. It is the males gathered around, all trying to be first or next or whatever, who make all the noise. Caterwauling is not sexual but aggressive. Such competitive din does not always result in actual fights because the males, however much they screech and carry on, are mostly fixated on the female who purrs and rolls on the ground, writhing and rubbing herself. The local male on whose territory the female has chosen to mate will typically go first, approaching the vamp and sitting close by. For this he is rewarded by slashing blows from her claws, and he hurriedly retreats. The local swain may not wind up being the first male to be accepted, but they all, when they make their approach, try to do so when the female is looking elsewhere. If she turns to look at an approaching male, he freezes. Eventually one male will get up close to her, emitting little chirping sounds, and she gives up hissing and spitting at him. He then is, for the moment, the chosen one.

All this sorting out can take hours, even days, the noisy rituals eventually overcoming the female's evident hostility to the entire process. The chosen male will then take the scruff of her neck in his mouth (which when mothers do it to kittens is a calming act) and carefully mounts her from behind, placing his forepaws on the ground beside her. If and when she is ready to copulate, she flattens her chest onto the ground, raising her rump with her tail to the side, and copulation occurs, lasting only a matter of seconds.

When it is over and the male withdraws from her, she lashes out, swiping at him with her claws. Why this last act takes place is no longer a mystery. The cat's penis has tiny keratin spines on

it that face backwards, so the withdrawal is painful enough to enrage the female. How this hard-to-think-about action would be adaptive, in the evolutionary sense, has been explained. For the female to ovulate, she needs to have some heavy-duty excitation, and the keratin spines seem to be just the thing. Even so, one would imagine that cat reproduction could, over the eons, have evolved into something less painful. (This is another of those little tricks of nature that gainsay the likelihood of intelligent design.)

In any event, the proceedings continue, the female copulating with several if not all the males in attendance, sometimes over a period of days. The males hang around, though they begin to tire of the whole affair, while the female writhes and rubs herself on the ground, redoubling her vamping to prolong the whole business. Eventually, her heat at an end, the males wander off and the female goes home.

Our friend Mary has provided insight on what at least one tomcat will do when both neutered and kept largely indoors and thus deprived of much in the way of sex. The tom is called DC by everyone; it stands for Damned Cat. Mary's husband didn't want a cat, though he came to be very fond of him. DC is not about to accept the life of the feline eunuch. Instead he will pester Mary until she unfolds a small blanket and places it upon a pillow on the sofa. DC then "has his way with his blankee," as Mary puts it. Not leaving it simply at that, DC (when he does manage to escape the house) gets into ferocious-sounding cat fights.

To the untutored human, cat sex may seem tawdry at best, and certainly a bit alarming in its raucous hostility. But as Abraham Lincoln noted, "No matter how much cats fight, there always seem to be plenty of kittens."

PART THREE
THE CAT'S WORLD

The world reaches a cat through its senses, which are both

windows and, as they connect to the brain, data processing

centers. And once these perceptions reach the brain,

they become the stuff of the cat's mind, a mysterious

presence indeed. The remaining chapters explore

that presence both indirectly and directly.

EIGHT-WEEK-OLD DELILAH, A GOOD TIME TO GO TO A NEW HOME.

Chapter 6
Kittens

The smallest feline is a masterpiece.
—LEONARDO DA VINCI

I f you were to bet someone that your female cat would give birth sixty-three days after she was impregnated, the odds are very good that you would win.

This is the same gestation period, by the way, that is common among dogs, and a few days longer than the gestation period of the domestic cat's progenitor, the African wild cat.

Biologists are inclined to look at newborn kittens not as young cats but something else—indeed, something metaphorically like the larval form of a butterfly that has to go through a considerable metamorphosis to become an adult. How can anyone call a little kitty, arguably the cutest animal on the planet, a larva?

In the first place, when born, a kitten cannot see. It takes up to a week or more for its eyes to start opening and another week or so to open all the way. By this time, the kitten has pretty good binocular vision and can visually follow some objects, like cats

or people. At about twenty-three days, the color of its eyes (typically blue at birth) will begin to change to their adult color.

The newborn kitten cannot hear, either. Its inner ears' early function, however—to give the animal a sense of balance—is already working. If you snatch up a little visionless and deaf newborn and place it on its back, it will thrash around in the interest of being upright, meaning stomach down, back up. But it cannot use its ears to hear until its outer ear canals open up, a process that starts at about nine days and is complete at seventeen. The kitten's sense of the world around it for these first two or three weeks then is limited largely to smell and touch and temperature.

A kitten's sense of smell is present at birth, and it is just about as sensitive as it will ever be by about three weeks of age. It is by smell (and also warmth) that a kitten orients itself to the mother's teats and, in fact, selects a favorite teat to which to make its way. It can paddle around a bit, using its front legs, and will head for warmth, particularly the warmth of its mother, and only with her help will it fasten onto the favored teat and suckle.

That is about all it can do—a larval sort of life. And this is a very good way of life for a newborn kitten. Among other things, its lack of total awareness of the world—a sudden glare of sunlight for example, or a loud noise, or the appearance of an enormous moving object such as a person—keeps the kitten from experiencing stresses it may not be neurologically or emotionally ready to experience. On the other hand, if one plays gently with these larval cats, it apparently can hasten the opening of their eyes by a day or so, which is evidently harmless. It can also help socialize the kitten to humans. Once beyond the larval stage, it takes some three months for the kitten's eyes to achieve their adult acuity, but in the meantime, kittens can make out their mother, their littermates, and other objects and creatures that enter their field of vision. The presence of light is essential in the development of sight: kittens raised in the dark will be functionally blind.

Sometime around nine days after birth, the kitten's ear ducts begin to open, a process that is complete by about the seventeenth day. By this time, the kitten will startle at sudden loud sounds, and after some three weeks or so, it can differentiate between its littermates or people by sound. At about this time, kittens begin to show a defensive maneuver—the arched back and hissing that will serve to warn enemies away—when confronted by threatening sights or smells.

Indeed, by three weeks, a big change has occurred. The larval kitten is well on its way to becoming a real cat. Its brain, which was only one-twentieth of adult weight at birth, is now at the adult weight (with a lot more neural connections to be forged, of course). Its milk teeth, those super-sharp baby teeth that can inflict a little bite on a finger as painful as a paper cut, are on the verge of being replaced by adult teeth. By the time another week or so passes, a free-ranging mother will begin to bring live prey such as mice to the kittens, and by the fifth week the kittens will start to kill the mice themselves. The kitten has passed from what is officially called its neonatal period (neonatal meaning essentially "new baby") to its next stage, called its sensitive period.

It is possible to make too much of these scheduled times. What is given here is the average age for certain developmental events to take place, but they can vary quite widely. For example,

some kittens' eyes begin to open as early as two days after birth, and some as late as sixteen days.

Scientific observers have succeeded in winnowing out four factors that seem to determine the onset of eye-opening in kittens. Those raised in the dark open their eyes earlier, and so do kittens of younger mothers. Also, females open their eyes earlier than males, as a general rule. But the most important influence seems to be how early the father's eyes opened—meaning that the most important factor is genetic, since kittens hardly ever even meet their fathers.

Do kittens whose eyes open earlier have a lifelong problem with the stresses of life—or less of a problem? The ability to handle various forms of stress with equanimity is an important factor in what might be called an animal's domesticatability, but it is hard to imagine that a few days one way or the other in the onset of eye-opening would have too profound an effect on a kitten's psyche. On the other hand, to begin to see where earlier all was dark, and to begin to hear where all before was silent, must be some kind of a shock to a larval kitten's system.

One thing is certain: there is a period of sensitivity in the early weeks of a kitten's life when it becomes socialized, meaning that it gets to be comfortable with the existence of other creatures besides its mother and siblings, such as humans or dogs. This sort of thing was first called imprinting. It arose from the study of birds, in particular geese. If, when the babies (called goslings) emerged from the eggs, they first saw a human rather than a goose, they would treat the human as if it were their mother; a famous photograph shows a single file of goslings waddling along after a male scientist, Konrad Lorenz. This identification seemed to take place immediately and irrevocably.

Meanwhile zookeepers had found that if they paid too much attention to baby gorillas, for example, hand-feeding them, as adults the gorillas would not be interested in mating with their own kind.

Later, scientists studying puppies found a "critical period" of eight weeks that began after week four, in which a puppy could be made comfortable with (socialized to) humans or other nondog species such as cats or sheep. After the twelfth week socialization was thought to be impossible and puppies that had not been socialized to, say, humans, would never be comfortable with them but instead be hostile or fearful. But it was then learned that even after the critical period, puppies could learn to accept humans (though it took more work), and so the name was changed to the "sensitive period." Such a period exists among kittens. It is a shorter period overall than for puppies, and it starts earlier, running typically from the end of two weeks of age to seven weeks.

Puppies do not require much more than a few minutes a day being handled by humans to become socialized to these huge two-legged creatures. On the other hand, kittens become far more comfortable with humans later in life if, during their sensitive period, they are handled some forty minutes a day or more. A few minutes here or there simply doesn't cut it. It turns out, too, that petting, playing with, and talking to kittens is more important than feeding them in establishing friendly relations. Kittens also are likely to distinguish children from adult humans, so it is best to have both handle a kitten.

The chief feeder and teacher of kittens—the mother—plays an important role here as well. The kittens tend to take their cue from the mother: if she is calm around humans, the kittens

are likely to follow suit. Similarly, if the mother is shy around humans, so her kittens will be, too. The calmness with which a cat confronts the world is essentially the lack of fear of new or minimally familiar things—a kind of boldness that will have a considerable effect on how comfortable a kitten will eventually be around humans or how curious and exploratory it will be. One has to wonder, as well, if a kitten's boldness might be related to how playful it will become, either with its littermates or its mother, or later with humans. Play among kittens and other animals is wondrous to see, easy to anthropomorphize (meaning attribute to impulses that are human), and not all that easy to explain by scientists who have looked into the matter. What purpose does play serve, either in terms of an individual kitten's development, or in the evolutionary terms of making a kitten a more successful adult cat that goes forth to reproduce itself? Complex, joyous, and still mysterious, play deserves (and receives herein) its own chapter.

In the meantime, it should hardly need to be said that the life of a kitten is inextricably tied to the mother—at least for several weeks. Then, typically some eight to ten weeks after birth, the weaning process heralds a significant change in the parent-offspring relationship. (Among cats, fathers have virtually no role besides impregnating the mother. Kittens tend to grow up in single-parent homes, and mother cats will repel any overtures on the part of the sire with what in some quarters is called extreme prejudice.) In the first weeks after birth, the mother will "present" herself to the hungry kittens, encircling them with her body and legs and lying on her side to permit the kittens to latch onto a nipple, pushing or pulling them to this desirable destination as needed. Soon a kitten undertakes the task of finding what may be its favorite nipple by itself and by the time the kitten is three months old, its mother's milk—however generously it still may flow—loses much of its nutritive value. Now the mother will typically become increasingly standoffish when importuned by her kittens, and will begin to leave the den and her kittens frequently in order to go hunting, bringing back dead prey animals like mice for the kittens to eat.

An interesting sidelight in feline maternal behavior is that many cats seem to be perfectly comfortable suckling another cat's kittens and the young of other species of animals, even those species that she will soon be bringing home to feed to her kittens. This rather ecumenical behavior is responsible for the endearing (or some would say creepy) photographs of mother cats suckling mice, puppies, and what have you. In a reversal of this, one of our daughters (also named Sally)—in a moment of celebration—obtained a two-month-old gray male kitten she named Cosmo and a three-year-old dachshund-sized and mostly Shih Tzu dog named Mona from the local animal shelter. Experts at the shelter explained that Mona had had at least one litter somewhere along the way, but they left her unspayed for the moment because she was suffering from a respiratory problem. Within days, Cosmo was importuning Mona for a little sustenance, and days later Mona was producing plenty of milk, her teats swelling up. Cosmo became a regular customer.

At the vet's suggestion, we brought Mona to our house to separate her from Cosmo, returning her after a couple of weeks had passed and her milk had dried up. Immediately Cosmo fell upon her and the milk came yet again. Cosmo grew to be almost twice the size of Mona, and the odd couple continued this behavior for several months. Exactly what evolutionary pur-

pose this served remains beyond any biological theories that I've ever heard of.

Instances occur where a mother cat will suckle her young until she is impregnated yet again, but typically the tug of war between kittens (who want milk) and mother cats (who have other things in mind) leads by the third month to an important learning situation for the kittens. They learn to become carnivores. The mother, as noted, brings dead prey animals back to the den, and the kittens learn to eat meat. Reason exists to think that the kittens will always favor that species (or those species) of prey that the mother introduces them to—sometimes to the exclusion of other perfectly good prey. The kittens may even make distinctions between two kinds of mouse or vole or rat. This has significant ramifications for people with kittens who grow up in an apartment or other isolation from the hunt. In not supplying dead (and later live) prey, the human mother-substitute can set the kitten on a narrow or broadly accepting lifelong taste trajectory. There is considerable evidence in favor of those who say their cat is a picky eater.

After a week or so of providing dead prey, the mother will return to the den with live prey—a mouse, say—and set it loose among the kittens. She will, once they have tried and failed to catch it, pounce on it herself, and make it available to the kittens. She continues to do this until the kittens can dispatch the mice themselves. Kittens mimic their mother in several important matters, and one would suppose that watching the mother pounce on a live mouse is the way a kitten learns to be its own hunter. But this is not necessarily so. Kittens taken away from the den before they have ever seen the mother hunt can, as adults, hunt perfectly adequately after a few solo tries. Hunting appears to be hardwired into the very soul of a cat, domestic and wild.

The hunting manner of the cheetah, as we have seen, is more complex and in a sense more technical than that of the other cats—the breathtakingly fast chase, hooking the prey with a dewclaw to knock it down. It seems that young cheetahs need to be taught, over several months at least, how to hunt before they go off on their own. Cheetahs were commonly used in Asia in earlier times in hunting, but it became clear that if they were removed from their mothers too early, they were inept hunters. And more and more evidence shows that male cheetahs spend a good deal of time together, gaining some advantage in the endless quest for prey on open land. Leopards, tigers, and jaguars all usually hunt in more closed quarters—forests, high grasslands, and so forth—where they can stalk their prey more easily, and thus they would derive no particular benefit from hunting in groups. Open land encourages group hunting, as in the lions' case of course, but evidence is accumulating that the groups of males can be as high as four, and from such gatherings the males derive some benefit, though exactly what benefit remains to be found out.

COSMO'S WHISKERS AND STARE.

Chapter 7

The Senses of Cats

It always gives me a shiver when I see a cat seeing what I can't see.

—ANONYMOUS

M y wife Susanne can look at a patch of clover in the lawn and, in minutes, pluck a four-leaf clover from all the rest. How she sees this so well is an utter mystery to me—and to her. It has to have something to do with pattern recognition but on a scale totally unfamiliar to me.

Similarly, just how another creature, a nonhuman creature like a cat, receives the world through its senses and into its brain is ultimately unknowable by humans, and probably not of any interest to the nonhuman animal such as the cat, who almost surely does not reflect upon such philosophical matters as the nature of reality. It simply receives the information from outside itself and acts upon it in the manner in which its brain directs. Cats, for example, are known to spend a good deal of time in the company of their familial humans simply staring off into the distance, apparently just chilling, their idle minds in neutral. But when you realize that cats have sharp periph-

eral vision, you become aware that your cat, even in its most idle waking moments, may well be watching you. The question then is what does the cat notice about you. What reality that you represent does the cat's senses absorb into its brain? The only way to start answering that question is to explore as best we can the several senses of cats, refined as they have been by millions of years of evolution to make possible, even successful, the life of a partly domesticated carnivore.

Another question to be asked, and hopefully answered, is how many senses cats actually have to perceive their world. The main five, of course—touch, smell, taste, sight, and hearing. But what of other senses often attributed to cats? If they have nine lives, could they have more than five senses? Do we ourselves have more than five? For example, lost cats have been shown with some scientific rigor to be able to find their way home from great distances. Is this a feline version of ESP, extrasensory perception? In fact, there is no such thing as perception that occurs without some sensory means of perceiving it. ESP simply stands for sensory tools possessed by a cat—or a medium—that work by some means that we don't yet understand. Until a few decades ago, no one knew that bats found their way around in the dark by ultrahigh-pitched sonar. No one knew until even more recently that elephants could communicate with each other over vast distances by vocalizations that are far lower than anything the human ear is designed to pick up. It seems that migratory birds can navigate huge distances from wintering to summering grounds by following the magnetic fields put forth by the earth itself. Can cats do that?

Touching

Any exploration of cat senses should begin with the first sense a cat itself is aware of—even in utero—the sense of touch, a sense that in some particulars at least is the easiest for a human to imagine. Any sense, broadly defined, is a combination of sensory nerves called neurons that receive and transmit a particular message, the nerves that carry the message to the brain, and the neurons in the brain whose job is to register the message and recognize its meaning. As anyone knows who has accidentally put a hand on a hot stove, the message from receptor to the brain and back to the hand travels at lightning speed. To act at such great speed, the neurons involved have to be covered with fatty sheaths called myelin, and among cats, the nerves for different senses become myelinated (and therefore fully functional) at different times.

The sense of touch begins to be functional some twenty or so days after conception—long before birth—and is well developed by birth. It involves various sensations—heat and cold, hard and soft pressure. A newborn kitten can find its mother's body heat by means of the heat sensors in the tip of its nose, the "leather," and this continues to increase in sensitivity into adult life, when cats can tell the difference between temperatures varying as slightly as one degree Fahrenheit. Paradoxically, in spite of such high sensitivity to temperature, a cat can sit without concern on a hot stove or near a fire in heat that is sufficient to singe its fur. Humans find skin temperature above about 112 degrees Fahrenheit extremely painful; a cat remains comfortable for another fourteen degrees. This relative imperviousness to heat on the part of a cat's nerve cells can lead to considerable

trouble once the cat is in the world of humans. No one knows how many cats sitting on the stove have caught on fire.

Some cats will ask for a bit of gentle stroking by rubbing themselves against the human's ankles, arching the back and raising the tail to the vertical. In a sense, petting a cat reminds it of the pleasurable sensation of being groomed by its mother when it was very young. But too much stroking is taken as threatening. Cats are not like dogs who will sit all day in one place as long as someone will scratch them. Not being especially social animals, cats typically will soon tire of being stroked and will leave, or flatten their ears menacingly, or even bite the hand that strokes them.

For furry animals in general, being stroked is almost surely a more intense feeling than it is for us furless humans—intensely positive or intensely negative. On a cat or a dog, for example, each hair grows out of a small cluster of cells that are fairly strongly tweaked when a hair has been moved. Each hair is like a lever, the shifting of which in one direction or another has a magnified effect on the sensory neurons at its base. The

WHISKER POSITIONS: AT REST (LEFT); WALKING (CENTER); GREETING, DEFENSIVE (RIGHT)

most sensitive levers on a cat's body are, of course, its whiskers, which scientists call vibrissae to differentiate them from a human's whiskers, which are just hairs growing out of the chin and face. These are especially thick and stiff hairs, and the little bundle of cells are three times farther below the skin than regular hairs. These deep cells send vibrissae-sensed messages

back to the brain along the same pathways as the nerves to the eyes. And some of them produce a sensation that is probably analogous to vision.

A cat has a large area on its upper lip plus a little area on its chin that are festooned with vibrissae. The upper-lip vibrissae are called mystacials, and there are twelve on each side of a cat's muzzle. They are carried in a forward position when the cat is about to kill a mouse or other prey. (Cats tend to be farsighted, and cannot see their prey when it is right before or under their noses. The mystacial vibrissae help out in this situation.) In addition, a cat has what are called superciliary vibrissal tufts over its eyes and genal vibrissae on its cheeks. Finally there are carpal vibrissae on the back of the cat's foreleg just above the paw. What these latter vibrissae are for is a bit of a mystery, perhaps helping with the capturing of prey or climbing trees.

The others—all on the face—are what have given the cat the reputation of being able to see in the utter dark. While the cat's eyes are excellent gatherers of light, even very low light, they cannot perceive anything in true dark. But the vibrissae, held forward, can detect the slightest motion of the air in a wide swath as wind or air currents are reflected from nearby objects—a kind of "seeing" that is unimaginable except perhaps to some blind people. Indeed, blind cats can fare quite well by using their whiskers to navigate around a room. The mystacial whiskers that emerge from their muzzle are typically long enough to equal the cat's body width, letting a cat know right away whether the opening to a small burrow or between a table's leg and the wall is big enough to slip through. (They don't provide this service for overweight cats.) A cat without its vibrissae is not likely to try hunting at night, a fact gleaned no doubt from

an old experiment that needs never be done again. Cutting off parts of animals for nonmedical reasons—even such seemingly insignificant parts as whiskers—strikes me as wicked.

One can easily imagine another sense that cats share with most other mammals, and perhaps other creatures, a sense that is different from touch in some ways, but also in some ways similar. It can be thought of as a kinetic sense, a sense of one's own body in action. Watch a cat stretching (or for that matter a dog, not to mention oneself). Clearly a pleasurable feeling goes along with it. I think back to my younger days and recall the usually pleasurable bodily sense of running flat out, jumping, serving a tennis ball, diving into water, shoveling dirt—extending myself physically in any number of ways and as often as not without any purpose whatsoever. It makes no sense to deny so pleasurable a physical sensation to an animal that can jump upward to a height five times its body's length, can run, pounce, and stretch so luxuriously, so smoothly as to appear to be made of liquid.

Smelling

The sense of smell is well developed by a kitten's birth. A couple of days later, the kitten will try to avoid an unpleasant odor and seek out a pleasant one—its mother, for example, and by day three, a particular nipple. Olfactory clues will add to the mother's bodily heat to serve as the means of locating not only a place to feed but the familiar home base in the event that the kitten strays. In three weeks or less, when the kitten's eyes are completely open, vision takes over as the primary means of navigating space. Until this occurs, a kitten's reliance on its nose can be dangerous. Kitten flu, which makes sniffing ineffective if not impossible, can prevent young kittens from finding a nipple to nurse.

For adult cats, judging whether a new place or a new cat is tolerable is in great part a matter of smells, certain of which—like the pungent odor of mothballs—will automatically send the cat into a rapid retreat. Greeting familiar cats also calls for an olfactory exploration, first face-to-face and then face-to-rear end, where anal sacs contain a variety of bacteria that give each cat an individual odor. And of course, as we noted in Chapter 5, smell plays a crucially important role in feline reproductive behavior and success. Like dogs and others, cats have a special organ for sniffing the chemical signals called pheromones—hormonally produced odors that signify such things as the oncoming heat of a female, an odor to which male cats are drawn like iron filings to a magnet. This special organ is called the vomeronasal organ; it lies inside the palate and is reached by canals that open just behind the incisor teeth. Its neural connections run via an accessory olfactory receiver directly to the amygdala, the part of the brain associated with sexual and aggressive behavior.

In response to the hormonal secretions that are processed in the vomeronasal organ, the cat raises its head, opens its mouth, and lifts its upper lip into what some people think of as a "sneer," the better to bring these delectable odors forcefully to bear. This posture is called *flehmen*, a German word for which there is no English translation, and flehmen occurs among various animals, including horses where it is especially elaborate and noticeable.

For a human being, imagining the intense sensations in-

volved in this specialized organ is impossible. And so is even the other, normal olfactory system of the cat. How indeed can one imagine the richness, or at least the extraordinary variety, of a cat's world of smells? To begin with, in the relatively short nasal area of a cat, the roof of the mouth is finely ridged to increase the actual amount of surface and contains three to six square inches of receptor cells. By way of comparison, we humans have some 20,000 olfactory cells (which is to say smell receptors), while a cat has some 67,000. This is more than three times the receptors given over to smelling things than we humans possess with our puny—one might even say poverty-stricken—sense of smell.

The molecules of incoming smells become attached to the cat's mucous cells and tweak the microscopic hairs in the cells, sending on an electric message to the brain via dedicated neurons. In addition, of course, the olfactory regions of the cat's brain are proportionately greater than ours.

Imagining the wealth of smells available to a cat's perception, as compared with our own, is made all the more impossible by the fact that smells, for us, are essentially evanescent. They come and go with each intake and exhaling of air through the nose. But cats (and dogs) have an additional olfactory structure in the nose: the hard-to-pronounce subethmoid shelf. Some of the odor-filled air the cat breathes does not leave the nose right away but instead rests upon this shelf for a brief period, allowing the cat (it is presumed) to study the odors, identifying each separately. For example, in the convenience store of a gas station near my house, a once-feral cat now sleeps behind the popcorn most days. The store has a familiar smell—a mixture of burritos, hot dogs, old wood floors, and so forth. The cat no doubt smells the burritos separately and the hot dogs, and the popcorn and the candy bars and the owners and the customers and so on . . . and on.

Tasting

Like smell, taste is another chemical sense, but one that is less developed in cats (and dogs) than in humans—at least based on the number and variety of receptor cells on our tongues. Cats have about half the taste buds on their tongues that humans with 9,000 possess. In this sense alone, humans exceed cats in acuity. Even so, cats have a reputation as finicky eaters. To switch a cat's diet—say, from dry food pellets to which the cat has become accustomed to the wet food that is healthiest for it (see Appendix B for important information on choosing cat food)— can be as discouraging as trying to get a human child, once tempted, to forswear junk food. It takes time and patience. Cats are inclined to prefer the food that their mothers (or humans) brought to them as they were being weaned. Whether this is a taste preference or one based on some other factor is not known, but making a change in a cat's diet is best done gradually.

Cats have been tested for overall food preferences, and the results differ from one test to another. In one trial, cats seem to prefer beef, lamb, horse meat, pork, chicken, and finally fish—in that order. In two other tests, however, cats preferred fish over meat. Yet another study showed when a cat is under a certain amount of stress or taken to a new house it will revert to eating only the food it was accustomed to as a kitten. It appears, in fact, that most cats are not put off by variety but will pick at and soon reject any food that is unpalatable to them.

Some house cats have trained their owners to provide a very narrow array of food under a tight series of procedures, and indeed what begins as a kind of cute prank for humans can become a hidebound tradition for the cat. A friend of mine in New York City, the mythologist and biographer David Leeming, has a beloved cat named Tita who will eat only when perched on an antique baby's high chair at the dinner table. David of course conspires in this odd behavior and in the behavior of an earlier cat member of his family, a female named Reggie (after the great baseball slugger, Reggie Jackson). Reggie insisted every day just before five o'clock in the afternoon that David and she go to his bedroom where he would lie down, Reggie would lie on her back next to him, and they would both listen to *All Things Considered* on National Public Radio. David is, of course, a sucker.

In any event, trying to explain what is palatable to cats in general runs a great risk of foolish error. However, a few things are known to be true in most cases. According to British veterinarian Bruce Fogle (see Further Reading), cats tend to prefer dense foods to lighter ones, whole milk to diluted milk, warm food rather than cold, and food that is slightly sour, bitter, or acid rather than sweet. Until recently it was believed that cats had no taste sensors for sweet things, but new studies show that there are areas in the cat brain that can distinguish sweet from other tastes, and the rule now is that cats show little natural preference for sweet foods. They can be trained to desire sweet-tasting foods, which are probably not all that good for a cat in the long run since they are not encountered in a wild cat's diet. Water is the best fluid to make available to cats unless they get sufficient water from wet meaty food. Young cats can drink milk, but as they age they tend to have a hard time digesting it.

One of the advantages to giving cats real meat to eat, aside from the basic needs of a strict carnivore, is that it contains an amino acid called tryptophan that helps to create serotonin, a brain hormone that affects sleep, wakefulness, and mood. Serotonin also appears to have the effect of inhibiting aggressiveness in cats.

One of the most astonishing animal–plant phenomena known is the connection between cats and catnip, also called catmint, and scientifically known as *Nepeta cataria*. Domestic cats are not alone in responding to it; lions, jaguars, leopards, and snow leopards are also aroused by catnip (but not tigers). In fact, about one in two domestic cats are not aroused by it. Probably a hallucinogen, it is sniffed by the cat, then licked, chewed, or eaten. In response the cat shakes its head; its back twitches. Holding on to some catnip in its paws, the cat rolls over on its side, wriggles and writhes, occasionally leaps, and in a general way acts as if it is in estrus. Other fairly common plants have similar effects: matatabi, valerian, cat thyme, and buckbean. So far, no one has reported any particular ill effects on cats who become catnip users, nor are there accounts of cats becoming addicted, though some scientists have suggested that catnip is not unlike LSD, promoting hallucinations. Another recent finding of considerable usefulness—though not to cats—is that catnip repels certain kinds of cockroaches.

Seeing

Cats have big eyes, and big eyes, as in babies, tend to be endearing to humans. Retaining babylike features is called neoteny, and it is an evolutionary "strategy" by which many domesti-

cated animals take advantage of the human being's emotional response to cuteness. In dog neoteny, this includes floppy ears held over from puppyhood and rounder eyes than those of a wolf. But the large eyes of cats are, however cute, technical marvels as well as the inspiration for an array of myths and legends. The primary myths associate the eyes of cats with the phases of the moon as it goes from full to a sliver and back, and thence to the tides. Given the cat's eyes' sensitivity to changing amounts of light, some cultures thought they served as adequate clocks, getting smaller as the sun moved up the sky and larger as it descended into dusk and darkness.

In biological terms the cat's eye is perhaps the finest possible compromise between the need to see in both the glare of high noon and the low light of a nocturnal hunt lit only by the stars. In this requirement, it is as effective as high-quality cameras. Cats cannot, as sometimes claimed, see in the absolute dark, but they can see when there is only one-sixth the amount of light in which the human eye can see. To us, that one-sixth is the practical equivalent of absolute dark. The cat's eyes are, to be precise, the best eyes evolution has yet created for the needs of a land-based nocturnal *and* diurnal predator.

To begin with, much like our eyes, they face the front with the two cones of sight overlapping considerably, providing depth perception (called binocular vision) over an arc of 120 degrees. Binocular vision is, of course, highly desirable for creatures who need to pounce on something the size of a mouse—or toss a large ball through a distant hoop as in basketball, or swing through the branches of a tree like a gibbon. A cat approaching its quarry will often move its head slightly from side to side making depth perception all the more accurate. The cat's prey, on the other hand, is better served by vision that provides as close as possible to 360 degrees of sight, and a mouse's eyes—or a Thomson's gazelle's or a rabbit's or most birds'—are located on the side of its head, permitting it to see most of the area behind it while providing it little or no binocular vision in the front. A cat can see laterally (with each eye) another 80 degrees, and has a blind spot behind them of 80 degrees. While this arrangement suits the cat as predator it is, like practically all anatomical features, a compromise in that domestic cats are preyed upon by the likes of coyotes if left out at night.

The precision with which a cat can see is very much the result of how the eye mimics the way a camera works—in particular, the way cameras worked that not only used that old-fashioned resource called film but were not fully automatic. The first thing a photographer with such a camera had to do was set the f-stop, which is to say the aperture or how wide open the camera aperture is. If it is dark, you want the aperture very large to let in a lot of what light is available; if it is very bright, you want the aperture shrunk down to a tiny hole.

In an eye—yours or a cat's—the black pupil is the part that lets the light come into the innards of the eye. In cats, the pupil when wide open can be as much as a half-inch in diameter. First, light comes through the mostly transparent cornea that focuses the light a little bit but mainly protects the eye from the outside world. Next is the iris, the colored part of your eye that opens up or closes down, arranging for the proper aperture size, which in your case or that of a dog, is a large or small circle. In a cat the iris moves laterally from the left and the right toward the center, producing an aperture shaped like a lozenge until it almost vanishes as a tiny vertical slit.

The cat's eye is subject to yet finer control by a membrane that moves from the inner corner of the eye across and down, turning the vertical slit into a tiny speck of black pupil (or closing the eye altogether). This is called the nictitating membrane and, in addition to giving yet further fine control over aperture (as do the eyelids), it also provides further protection of the eye from damage by the outside world. You yourself have the evolutionary remnant of a nictitating membrane: the little triangular piece of skin in the inner corner of each eye.

This then is the basic plan of all cat eye aperture setting, big and small, except for two species, lions and the Pallas's cat, a small, stout cat of the Central Asian steppes and desert, whose eyes have irises that create *round* apertures like yours or your dog's. Lions are diurnal hunters and don't need so rapid a response to sudden blinding light, but the Pallas's cat is nocturnal and why its eyes have round apertures is simply not clear. Whatever the evolutionary advantage (or lack of disadvantage), the round pupils give Pallas's cat a bug-eyed manic look.

That a black pupil, which looks like nothing less than a piece of highly polished opaque obsidian, is the light-gathering medium seems strange enough. Behind the pupil lies one of the most remarkable organs in biology, a crystalline lens capable of focusing the incoming light onto the "film," which is to say the light-sensing cells of the retina that lie over the back of the eye. The image that the lens refracts onto the cat's retinal cells is about five times brighter than the image your eye can form—but the image is not as sharp as ours.

PALLAS'S CAT

In order to focus light on the retina, the lens changes shape through the action of a host of tiny muscles, a process called accommodation, and human eyes do this twice as well as cats, thus providing most humans with the sharper image that permits, say, reading the second to last line on the optometrist's eye chart until you are sixty or seventy years old when your accommodation muscles flag. Cats do not need to read tiny objects, but they have a great need to track movement. Their eyes are designed to meet this more important need. If the cat's central image is not so sharp as ours, their peripheral vision is considerably clearer. More often than not, cats observe the world around them via the periphery of their vision, making them seem aloof to some observers, but as the ethologist Konrad Lorenz noted, when a cat looks directly at something, it is likely to be up to "no good." In this regard, cats rarely stare at one another unless a fight is in the offing.

So given to perceiving motion are cats that utterly naïve kittens will automatically chase anything that moves across their line of sight or away from them—such as mice or mechanical mice or a rolling ball of yarn. In an experiment, naïve kittens would only stare at mechanical mice that ran around in circles or moved erratically. Only after the mechanical mice ran down and appeared therefore to be dead would the kittens approach to sniff them.

The photoreceptor cells that line the eye's retina come in two basic kinds—rod-shaped cells and cone-shaped cells. Rods respond to small amounts of light, while the cones respond to bright light and with far greater acuity than rods. It takes a lot of rods to turn a tiny amount of light into something meaningful; a cat has twenty-five rods for every cone: in all, each eye has millions of these unimaginably tiny receptors. When light strikes them it is turned into chemical energy, then electrical energy, and conveyed to the brain by special optical nerve cells or neurons.

The image created in the brain by rods is a continuum of

gray, ranging from black to white. The brain's gray image is the result of a lot of rods transmitting information via a given optical neuron. This is a good system for bringing about an image in very low light, but it makes it impossible to tell exactly where the detail is coming from. Thus the image is not totally sharp.

On the other hand, each cone conveys its information to a single neuron, providing a very sharp image in the brain. The other important thing about cones, of course, is that they respond to specific wavelengths of light, which is to say colors. Thus, cats do see color, greens and blues. Not much, then, and not anything like the intensity of color that we humans see, but some. Cats can be trained (arduously, it turns out) to act upon color distinctions, but such distinctions do not seem to play much of a role in normal cat behavior.

On the upper half of the cat's retina is a triangular patch of cells that are crystalline in nature and contain bits of zinc and riboflavin. This patch is called the tapetum lucidum, and it acts as a mirror in the back of the cat's eye, reflecting what light the eye has not absorbed back through the system. The result is the manner in which cat's eyes shine at night, a light compared to the sparkle of diamonds, a revival of the light they have absorbed during the day, or ominously the night shine that arises from the devil's fires. It is not uncommon among many nocturnal animals—deer caught in headlights are one of the most common versions—but among cats the light is especially intense. In cats with copper or gold eyes, the light reflected back is a yellow-green or blue-green. In blue-eyed cats, the night shine is red.

Hearing

The second most important sense for a nocturnal hunter, hearing is carried on in cats and other animals in a system that originated far earlier in the course of evolution and for an entirely different function. Called the vestibular system, it helped animals sense if they were not upright. This is particularly well developed in cats and is an important feature in the cat's ability to land on its feet, a legendary bit of cat behavior that is probably the most popular "scientifc experiment" performed by small boys, and not always with happy results. How many cats have been experimentally tossed out of second-story windows in the name of science? Enough for some veterinarians to refer to "flying cat syndrome," typically an urban phenomenon.

Deep in the cat's ear are several fluid-filled chambers, each lined with millions of tiny hairs. Two of the large chambers also contain tiny crystals of calcium carbonate that tend to fall onto whatever hairs are at the bottom at any given moment. This sends signals with terrific rapidity to a part of the brain given over to coordinating up or down orientation. In addition, three fluid-filled canals that are placed at right angles to one another signal the brain about what direction the cat is headed in and how fast it is speeding up.

When a cat is picked up by the legs and held upside down over a bed (one hopes) and let fall, even if it is only three feet above the bed, it will manage to wriggle around in time to land on its feet. Part of the reason it can do this is the speed with which its vestibular system lets it know where down is; the rest is a result of the almost liquid plasticity of the cat's backbone. A cat's vertebrae are more loosely connected than most animals'.

When dropped, the first adjustment is the leveling of the cat's head. Then with its back legs still pointing up, its front legs and the front half of its body spin 180 degrees (see drawings). The back end then twists around as well, and with its back arched to help accommodate impact, the cat lands on its four feet. Cats can typically fall up to two stories and still withstand the impact, but over two stories will cause injuries, particularly to the cat's head. At four stories, the injuries become even more severe, damaging internal organs and causing death.

Oddly enough, some cats survive falls of over seven stories and veterinarian Bruce Fogle points out that this is because a fall of that height takes enough time for the cat to relax, spread its legs and, somewhat in the manner of a flying squirrel, glide to a safe landing. The cat's forelegs are not tightly attached to a collarbone like ours but have free movement that allows them to walk with one foot in front of the other and also to more easily absorb impact from jumping or falling down, even occasionally from great heights. No one, however, is encouraged to duplicate any of these adventures in the name of science or anything else.

The vestibular system began with the first fish, and in cats it is as highly refined as in any animal. That its basic form and function evolved from fishy beginnings into the system by which animals collect and derive meaning from sound is one of the astonishing stories of evolutionary creativity and fine-tuning, a matter of uncounted and uncount-able steps made over millions of years that were surely imper-ceptible from generation to generation.

Like light, sound travels in waves, but sound waves are not made up of photons in motion but rather molecules of air that are pressured by events to move. The tree that falls in the forest, crashing to earth, creates a tremendous force on the surround-ing air, sending molecules outward, pressing against other air molecules that shove yet other air molecules and so forth until they reach an ear. If they don't reach an ear, they are not heard, for all their real physical existence.

Sound waves are measured in cycles per second—which is to say, how many times in each second does the wave go from the bottom to the top. This is called the sound wave's frequency. The fewer cycles per second, also called hertz (Hz), the lower the sound. The more cycles per second, or hertz, the higher the sound. Humans generally hear a range from 20 Hz, which is like the lowest note a bass player can make, to 20,000 Hz, which is about three octaves above the highest note on a piano. In our human-oriented way, we call anything below 20 Hz in-frasound, while anything above our high of 20,000 Hz is called ultrasound.

Some of a tiger's roar occurs in infrasound. Elephants com-municate over great distances in infrasound; no one knew that until recently when researcher Katherine Payne was in a zoo's elephant house and *felt* (not heard) the whole place vibrating. Bats emit sonarlike noise as high as 100,000 Hz by which they navigate in the dark, and dolphin sonar takes place even higher. Domestic cats may hear a little way down into infrasound, but for survival purposes they need to hear at least as high into

ultrasound as 50,000 Hz, which is the level of some but not all mouse squeaks. Some mouse squeaks are yet higher, in the 95,000 Hz range. Cats probably have the actual equipment to hear at 100,000 Hz, but for all practical purposes, the highest that is usual is about 50,000 Hz.

In addition to frequency, there is intensity or loudness. This is measured in decibels; zero decibels is the quietist sound a human can hear. A hundred decibels, on the other hand, denotes a sound so loud that it can be painful and will, if repeated often enough, do damage to the human ear. Millions of young peoples' and older peoples' ears have been permanently damaged by extra-loud music, not to mention the screeching of subway trains, the roaring of trucks in city streets, and other noise of our industrial and electronic world. One can imagine that a cat, with ears quite a bit more sensitive than ours, must be devastated by the sounds of civilization. It is, in fact, not at all uncommon for older cats to lose their hearing acuity, just as humans do.

When sound waves do reach the neighborhood of a cat's ear, the cat will use twelve muscles each to swivel its ears toward the sound waves. Cats can almost instantaneously tell the direction a sound is coming to within about five seconds of arc. This ability is largely a question of how far apart the ears are, and humans (having bigger heads) can distinguish a sound's direction to some three seconds of arc.

Once captured in the cat's radar antenna–like ears, sound waves pass downward until they reach the eardrums, which vibrate at approximately the same frequency as the incoming sound. These vibrations are passed on to the inner ear where, in a liquid-filled chamber, three tiny bones—known colloquially as the hammer, anvil, and stirrup—vibrate and turn the physical action into electrical impulses via the millions of tiny hairs in the chamber, and these electrical impulses go from thence through auditory neurons to the brain.

ESP

People of a scientific turn of mind tend to be pretty skeptical about ESP or extrasensory perception. They say that if any kind of perception takes place, it has to be as a result of some sensory receptor getting a message from out there in the world or somewhere in the brain. For example, people studying elephants (from a huge distance) had seen that two separate herds of elephants that were many miles apart would sometimes simultaneously change direction and head for each other. This remained mysterious and unexplained until Dr. Payne ascertained that elephants could communicate by infrasound—and since infrasound wavelengths have very low frequency, meaning that each cycle is very long, they don't all get fouled up in the trees and brush like short waves. Instead, some infrasound waves will go around such obstacles and so can travel long distances.

Elephants didn't have ESP; they had infrasound.

So how do some cats seem to have little trouble getting around even if they are deaf? Aside from the use of their whiskers, it is speculated that their feet are so sensitive that they can pick up the vibrations on the floor, say, of someone walking in a familiar gait. Many cats will also run to the door a few minutes before their human walks in, predicting their arrival. Cats have a biological clock that is fairly accurate about the passage of

twenty-four hours, so they know what is likely to happen if they live in a household with regular comings and goings. Also, they can hear sounds you and I cannot, and can learn to distinguish the sound of your car engine from others, or your footsteps on the stairs.

What is harder to explain is the cat's legendary capability to find its way home from long distances. Stories abound of such miraculous navigation, among dogs as well as cats, but cats seem more given to these feats. And indeed, some scientists have made detailed and rigorous studies of this phenomenon among cats and have convinced themselves that these are not just odd anecdotes but definitely a real phenomenon, a pattern of behavior. Just what senses the cat is using remains speculative. It could be that cats, like birds, can sense the magnetic field of the earth itself and follow its directions to home. It isn't a matter of memory, since such journeys are often as the crow flies.

As for cats (and other domestic animals) going nuts before earthquakes, the fact is they don't always react in any visible way, so they don't seem to be particularly reliable predictors of quakes. On the other hand, if their feet are sensitive enough to serve as an alternative to hearing, who is to say that they don't sense some early onset of a quake? Most geophysicists, however, are inclined to prefer seismometers, lasers, and other sensing equipment.

Anyway, cats have plenty to do without being enlisted to take care of geological catastrophes. One account of an utterly extraordinary sensitivity tells of a cat named Oscar who lives in a Providence, Rhode Island, nursing home. Evidently Oscar, who was not especially fond of the patients in general and rarely if ever visited them, would curl up in the bed of a patient who was about to die. Oscar, the home claimed, had been correct in twenty-one occasions. No one has any explanation for Oscar's odd ability, but the medical people at the home have speculated that it has to have something yet to be detected to do with the cat's sense of smell and the person's pheromones.

PLAYFUL ATTACKS COME NATURALLY TO DELILAH.

Chapter 8
The Mysteries of Play

Do you see that kitten chasing so prettily her own tail? If you could look with her eyes, you might see her surrounded with hundreds of figures performing complex dramas...

—RALPH WALDO EMERSON

One of the more attractive features of play, whether carried on by a cat, a dog, a human, or even a turtle, is what appears to be its essential carefree frivolity. Explaining or analyzing play was long avoided by biologists, mainly because it seemed to take place without any direct purpose or benefit to the animal. It wasn't clear that playing made an animal fitter to survive. It just seemed like some sort of extraneous activity—behavioral white noise.

Two millennia ago, Plato took note of the tendency of young animals including young humans to leap playfully in the air. He theorized that young animals needed a great deal of exercise, and in using up energy, gained endurance and the skills necessary for an adult life. Two thousand years later, most scientists who have thought about such things had taken the matter no further.

"Behavioral fat," some called play dismissively. A way of

filling spare time when important matters were not pressing, was another rationale. An actual named theory arose in the late 1980s—the Surplus Resource Theory. Well-cared-for captive animals, for example, might be expected to play more than animals in the wild, since captives have all of their physical needs more than amply taken care of—especially food.

Still, play seemed mostly senseless and certainly not functional in any sort of evolutionary role in the animal's life. What evolutionary advantage could it bestow? What biological consequences did it provide besides running the risk of getting hurt? Therefore, play was not a phenomenon that biologists could usefully study. And there was another reason why play was neglected. It was a trap, waiting to plunge biologists into considerations that had to be lacking anything solid. In other words, play looked like fun. And fun was a slippery concept—an invitation to anthropomorphize lower animals, to attribute to them humanlike qualities of mind that could not be proved.

A kitten batting a ball of yarn around the room sure looks like fun. To see two ravens doing synchronized barrel rolls as they plunge into an updraft is to see two ravens having what sure looks like fun. Puppies roughhousing, rolling around and jumping on each other, certainly suggests the same kind of fun little boys have when they do the same thing. But fun was long considered an exclusively human emotion (along with many other emotions). No way existed to determine scientifically if animals possessed such emotions.

Indeed, if animals like cats, dogs, even chimpanzees (our closest genetic relatives) had any emotional lives at all, they were thought to be characterized by such basic urges as anger, fear, hunger, and sex. Otherwise, such animals were little more than organic robots following behavior patterns laid down by their genes, their brains developing according to strict and un-avoidable rules set forth by their DNA. Human emotions like happiness, fun, affection, and embarrassment were beyond an-imals. That was because, it was believed, animals did not have the sort of self-awareness that psychologists and philosophers insist underlie such emotions. Enjoyment—and its opposite, suffering—if it existed at all in the psyche of cats and dogs and other animals, was extremely primitive, and therefore not really important. Dogs, for example, could be taught to salivate at the ringing of a bell once the scientist (in this case Dr. Pavlov) had taught them to associate the bell with the smell of meat. In other words, some animals could learn by what is called the conditioning of response.

And that was that.

A kind of educational component of play was noted, of course: a kitten or a puppy engaging in roughhouse with another was probably getting the hang of pushing others around (or submit-ting) in the great pecking order of life that faced them. When young ravens dive-bombed young wolves in a boisterous game of catch-me-if-you-can, they might be exuding a bold, risk-taking aura that would attract females once everyone grew up.

A lone kitten stalking a toy, pouncing on it, and then biting it was presumably in some way learning how to hunt. That was all straightforward, pretty cut-and-dried. But, in the 1980s a lead-ing biologist of animal behavior, Donald Griffin, published a book called *Animal Intelligence*. The book set most animal be-haviorists' teeth on edge, but it had to be taken a bit seriously because Griffin was a superlative researcher. It was he who had discovered that bats get around by means of echolocation (that

is, animal sonar), and he had taken up the mystery of bird migration in a direct way—that is, by flying alongside them in an airplane.

In any event, biologists began openly discussing and studying the minds of animals, and looking at play behavior in a new light. One of the scientific institutions that took a lead in this newly recognized realm was the Smithsonian's National Zoological Park, which held a series of seminars and scientific gatherings on the mental life of animals including the exploration of what animal play was all about. New kinds of questions could be asked.

A kitten, for example, will often approach a littermate or its mother, and lie down on its side in front of her. This posture is a cat's invitation to play, and a little bit of roughhouse follows. Or the mother will tweak the tip of her tail in front of a kitten who thereupon pounces on it. Kittens thus learn the moves involved in hunting and fighting. But what about adults playing, which they occasionally do? Presumably they already know how to hunt and how to engage in actual agonistic behavior (i.e., fighting). When a kitten batted a ball of yarn or some other object around, that looks a lot like learning how to vanquish a prey animal. But it turns out that such object play simply isn't necessary for a cat to learn the moves in catching prey. Just seeing its mother (or some other adult cat) catch a mouse once is enough for a kitten to know how to go about it; there are plenty of instances where kittens, reared without adult cats present, get pouncing on prey right all by themselves after only a few botched efforts. In matters of predation, the learning curve of young cats is approximately vertical, which is to say that it is probably a largely innate response to micelike objects on the move.

The context in which play takes place is important. For example, adult cats will resort to playful behavior if they confront an animal, such as a really big rat, that they are afraid of. What is the cat accomplishing by this?

An ethologist, Maxeen Biben, suggests that there are several possible explanations here. A cat that is unfamiliar with a new prey animal may use play to familiarize itself with the animal. Or play might serve to increase the cat's motivation to kill the prey animal. Or it may frighten the new prey animal and make it easier for the cat to subdue it. Or, one must suppose, some or all of the above, or maybe none. In other words, we don't know what it is all about.

Kittens playing—by themselves or with others—is surely the cutest thing anyone will ever see. Indeed, anyone who can watch this behavior without a smile probably needs to jack up his or her antidepression meds. (Susanne points out that one reasonable exception to such adoration is a knitter. The tiniest kitten can turn a ball of yarn into a tangle of mythological complexity.)

Such cuteness, however, is possible only after the kitten has reached a few developmental milestones. To begin with, it has to be at a point where it can accurately put its paws in a place that its eyes dictate, and this place is often a moving target, calling for considerable eye-paw coordination. In order for the eyes to lead the paws properly to the goal, the kitten's neck has to be able to maintain the head as a solid and level platform for the eyes so that the motion of the object to be played with (chased, swatted, pounced on) can be properly tracked. A more dramatic example of this can be seen in films of cheetahs chasing down their prey. The cheetah, racing along at sixty or seventy miles an hour, may have to make several sharp turns, each one calling for the body to lurch to the side, kept upright by (among other things) the cheetah's long tail reaching out as a counterbalance. Indeed, the entire body—limbs, tail, backbone—will be in constant motion, except the head, which remains still as a rock so that the eyes, kept on a horizontal plane, can constantly gauge the prey's motion.

CHEETAH

Currently, it appears to be generally accepted that animal play serves to encourage the expansion of neural connections in the young mammal's brain that permit such important features as eye-paw coordination and the kinds of kinetic sense of the body-in-action that any cat or dog or other type of athlete will need in life. Play can be thought of, perhaps, as brain food. Indeed, it has been found that puppies who do not have the opportunity to play wind up with smaller brains than those who do play. The same is surely true of kittens.

Is this also the function of what some cat specialists call "hallucinatory" play? This is when a kitten (or a cat) takes off in a chase . . . of nothing. Or races around batting at . . . nothing. Leaping, pouncing on nothing. What do the precepts of animal behavior have to say about this? In fact, very little. Along with the question of why cats tend to play with their prey, batting a dead or nearly dead mouse around, for example, hallucinatory play remains and may well remain indefinitely another of the mysteries that cats and their lives present to the world.

On the other hand, to return to a mode of inquiry more like science, one way to look at the playful behavior of kittens is to ascertain what happens if a kitten grows up without playing. If there is only one kitten in a litter, the mother cat will spend a good bit of time playing with it, taking up the slack, as it were. Hallucinatory play may well be the expression of an exuberant physicality in the absence of playmates or play objects—which is to say, a lack of stimulation, also known as boredom. Lacking all remedies, if a kitten is withdrawn from its mother and litter-mates before it has developed sufficient mental and muscular control for play, it will very likely grow up to be nervous, even hostile to other cats and other creatures including humans. Miserable, in other words.

Writer Stephen Budiansky, an insightful chronicler of the character of cats, dismisses most explanations for the play of cats, suggesting that in the long run it is simply what cats, and especially kittens, do. Not every single thing an animal does, he believes, has to be recorded as an asset or a liability in the Great Ledger of Evolutionary Adaptation. Budiansky shares this belief with the writer Garrison Keillor of Lake Wobegon, who says "Cats are intended to teach us that not everything in nature has a function."

Finally, play is clearly part of the young animal's growth and development (including young human animals), and one would have to be more grouchy than Dr. Seuss's Grinch to watch kittens, puppies, children, or other young animals play and refuse to admit that they are also having fun. That the emotion of kitten fun may differ in unfathomable ways from human kid fun is altogether possible and even likely, but after generations of scientists have denied any form of human-type emotions to animals, that wall has essentially crumbled. A law that scientists like to invoke is called Occam's Razor, based on the thoughts of a Franciscan monk known as William of Occam who taught philosophy in fourteenth-century Oxford. It says that the simplest explanation that fits all the facts is probably the most accurate. That human play is fun is obvious, and that kitten play brings on some kind of kittenish version of fun may be the simplest way to explain it.

SALLYANN HAD THE MOST PARTICULAR TASTE IN MUSIC.

Chapter 9

How Cats Communicate

The cat only grinned when it saw Alice. It looked good-natured, she thought: still it had very long claws and a great many teeth, so she felt that it ought to be treated with respect.

—Lewis Carroll

Early one morning in Washington, D.C., a long time ago, my wife and I approached a metal door that led into the Lion House of the Smithsonian's National Zoological Park, where we had been invited to experience an amazing event. I could feel the metal doorknob vibrating in my hand, and when we opened the door and walked in we were surrounded with the unholy sound of lions and tigers roaring for their breakfast. The sound was all-encompassing—something, I imagined, like drowning in a flash flood.

Scientists refer to such sounds as vocalizations, part of their cool and objective lingo designed to damp emotion, that enemy of rational thought, but to me this cacophony was the scariest thing I had ever heard. The writer David Quammen, in his book *Monster of God*, speaks eloquently of the special place in the panoply of human fears that the appetites of the big cats inspire even today—the terror of being eaten is evidently something elemental for us descendants of the early Stone Age when

humans were fair game for the likes of leopards, lions, and
tigers.

On this day at the zoo, the great cats were in cages of what
seemed to me pretty flimsy wire; I noted that a tiger, eyes flash-
ing, was rattling his cage approximately three inches away from
my leg, and I could barely hear the metallic crashes over the
roaring. White fangs glistened only a foot or so away. Some
eight or nine hundred pounds of bone and muscle encased in
orange and black fur rippled hugely. Some of the roaring was
clearly infrasonic, too low to actually hear but surely accounting
for much of the vibratory ocean I seemed to be in. All in all, a
bracing experience, all the more so as each big cat received its
huge slab of beef and the sound of row after row of carnassial
teeth slicing the juicy raw meat replaced the tsunami of pantherine roars.

What was it all about? The great ethologist George Schaller
found that lions roar when they are trying to assemble the
pride. But the lions present that morning were already as-
sembled in pretty close quarters. And lions are, of course, the
only truly social cats. Then what are the tigers, known soloists,
doing joining in the chorus? Could all that roaring be just plain
old excitement? Who knows? Is roaring an enjoyable feeling
or an unpleasant strain on the throat? In fact, when it comes
to the many ways that both wild and domestic cats communicate—and in spite of a good deal of study—a lot remains to
be understood (which is good news for the next generation of
zoologists).

Far more than the roaring of the great pantherine lineage,
however, purring and miaowing are the most familiar cat vocalizations. A cat owner hears these sounds often through the day.
(Another familiar cat sound, of course, is the yowling that ac-

companies mating but that, happily, is not usually a daily plague for people.) We go now from the fearsome to the sublime.

Evidently all cat species purr and only domestic cats miaow. Until a couple of decades ago, nobody knew exactly how cats purr, nor did anyone know what it was for except as an expression of contentment. That certainly was a strange lapse in the investigation of cat communication. After all, what noise emitted by any animal, wild or domestic, is more pleasing, more salutary to the human psyche, than the purring of a cat who has curled up on one's lap? Indeed, purring has been implicated in various beneficial psychological effects (mostly simple calming as in the healing of broken hearts) and its sound frequencies are claimed to be just right to heal broken bones.

Before we get to all that, we pause here to report on what to some might be an interesting philosophical debate among animal behaviorists about the nature of animal communication, particularly vocal communication. If you find philosophical disputes boring you are, of course, invited to skip the next paragraph and resume reading with the one that starts "So what about purring?"

The philosophical question is twofold at least. First, is information, a real identifiable and discrete packet of data as it were, embodied in a vocal animal call (such as a miaow)? Or is the cat's miaow merely an emotional and not really deliberate expression of the cat's state of mind? In this case, the miaow may simply add a new dimension to the overall environment that other cats can attend to or not as they see fit. Second, if the miaow of Cat A does embody a discrete clump of data, does that miaow mean exactly the same to Cat B who hears it? At some level, such considerations can clarify what exactly is going on in the communication of animals. Both questions are

confused, philosophically at least, by the many meanings of the word "communication." How active is it, how deliberate? After all, two rooms with a door leading from one to the other are communicating rooms in spite of the fact that nothing much is happening. These things can get wonderfully complicated and occupy the minds of people who might otherwise get in some kind of trouble, so we needn't laugh at them. My inclination is to think that some biologists get too hung up on information theory and see it everywhere, while all animals besides humans really don't use information as such, but instead emit emotional outbursts that are effective but not really deliberate, in the sense of an animal's saying to itself "That animal's presence makes me mad, so I will roar with anger and see if that animal understands me." The debate over this issue will continue and maybe one day even be resolved.

So what about purring? It is accomplished during both inhaling and exhaling and, except for a tiny pause between inhale and exhale, it seems to most human ears as continuous. What is happening is that the muscles of the larynx move the glottis (the area where the vocal cords are) on a cycle of contraction and release every thirty or forty milliseconds. The pressure and release on the glottis closes it and opens it, which makes the vocal cords generate the humming sound.

What is it for? Most purring seems to be a sound of contentment. Kittens can purr at birth, and they do so when suckling, which in turn may have the effect of keeping the mother there nursing. This is what scientists sometimes call an affiliative signal—one that keeps two individuals together. Adult cats may build on this infant effect as they purr when in contact with familiar cats (or humans). They also will often purr when "affiliating" with inanimate objects, like when they roll around on the rug or rub themselves on chair legs or what have you. These are all surely pleasurable situations, but veterinarians have found that when they are trying to repair cats who have suffered some physical trauma or extreme psychological stress, the cats will often purr. Surely they are not happy. Speculatively, when a distraught or injured cat purrs, it may be seeking a way to calm itself.

Purring is in one of three categories of cat sounds, according to the well-known vet Michael Fox, who wrote the preface for this book. Along with the soft sounds for greeting one another, purring is what Fox calls a murmur—sounds made with the mouth shut. High-intensity sounds—made with the mouth open—are used in most communication with other cats: growls, wails, snarls, hisses, spitting, and shrieks of pain. All of these sounds, both vocal and nonvocal, are impelled by what might be thought of as fear or anger. The third category is what Fox calls vowel sounds—notably but not only the miaow. (In fact, most mammalian—and avian—vocalizations are vowel sounds only. The cat's lips are simply not able to press together like ours when we pronounce *M*. The cat is really saying "iaow" and our ears, so attuned to consonant sounds, stick the *M* in there when we try to mimic a cat.) The cat's vowel sound calls are used to ask for something, to complain about something, or to express confusion. In these instances, the cat's mouth stays open, changing shape to make different vowel sounds.

Miaowing, indeed, comes in many forms and can turn into a fairly rich array of sounds devoted to getting humans to do something. Kittens have their own version of a miaow, employed when they are cold, hungry, or otherwise in some distress, such as when their mother inadvertently lies on them. Adult cats seldom miaow to each other but employ it to in-

fluence the behavior of humans, varying the intensity of the miaow depending on the circumstances. When it means "open the door, I want to come in," it will go from relatively soft to very loud and quite harsh, even unpleasant-sounding, depending on how long the human fails to pay attention. By twelve weeks old, a kitten can make all of these sounds—the vocal ones as well as the nonvocal ones, but how complex their range of miaows will get depends on their social circumstances. Recently Nicholas Nicastro, a graduate student at Cornell University, analyzed the miaows of cats and of the African wild cat that gave rise to the domestic cat. The African wild cat's calls were neither pleasant nor appealing. Instead the wild cats sound permanently and perpetually angry. It must have been unusually pleasant-sounding wild cats that joined up with humans all those thousands of years ago, and in the interval domestic cats, impelled by artificial selection, developed a wide array of miaow sounds, the better, one assumes, to control humans.

Some cats have been found to take vocal sounds even further, producing different sounds for "mouse" and for "rat." The mouse call tends to be a quiet, high-pitched gurgle but the rat call is more of a scream. Why? Possibly because mice are, so far as the cat is concerned, harmless, while rats can be dangerous. Kittens respond to these two calls as you might expect. They rush to find the mice but approach the rat with considerable caution. That sounds just a little bit like protowords, and you can start one hell of an argument full of human growls and hisses in the local university if you claim these vocalizations are something like words. The current dogma is that only apes and monkeys come close to using words.

A major mode of feline communication is via the sense of

smell, and for many cat owners this can be a bit of a problem, for the most odiferous (to us) and probably the most effective means of olfactory communication is via cat urine. Male cats are the most frequent users, but all females use it as well, especially when coming into heat. When a cat is simply relieving itself, it will squat down, much in the manner of a female dog. But when a cat is trying to say something, it will back up to a vertical surface (a tree or bush or a sofa will do), raise its tail straight up, and spray—a practice that is universal among cat species.

Our friend Mary has another cat besides DC—Mac—who demonstrated another use for spraying urine. He was at one time accustomed to prowling the neighborhood freely, but a neighbor began assaulting cats who wandered into his yard. Mary set about building a huge outdoor cage for Mac and her other cats so they could be outdoors without danger. Mac did not take well to his imprisonment. He would approach Mary and get her attention and, while staring directly into her eyes, spray mightily on the furniture nearby. Cat anger? Cat revenge?

It is said that neutering household cats can reduce much spraying behavior if not eliminate it, but smelling this signal is no big challenge even to the poor sense of smell that humans possess. If friends visiting a house that is occasionally treated to this pungent aroma make a face or object, there is not much one can do about it. Possibly one might deflect such rude opprobrium by saying something like, "Oh, yes. That's felinine and isovalthene, you know, special amino acids that show I give my cat high-quality food." Failing that, which is likely, the only real resort is to limit one's friendships to other, understanding animal people.

In any event, most cats (especially wild ones but many domestic ones) live in a world of scents left by other cats. Some scents are excretory; others are glandular secretions most of which humans cannot discern with their noses. A cat has a remarkable array of glands that can leave behind a calling card. For example, special glands are found between the toes of cats that presumably leave some meaningful identification on the places that cats scratch. The scratching (again a bit of a problem in a home unless a proper scratching post is supplied) is not to sharpen the claws but must have something to do with conditioning them. And whatever scent is left behind by the interdigital glands is unknown for the very reason that no one has observed other cats sniffing such places.

Similarly, a cat's head is an array of glands—under the chin, on the corners of the mouth, and on each side of the forehead. Cats do a lot of head-rubbing on objects, other cats, and humans. It seems to most humans to be a sign of comfort and even affection on the part of the cat, but humans cannot smell these secretions and evidently no one knows exactly what they accomplish in catdom. There is some speculation that—at least among groups of feral cats—they may serve to produce a characteristic smell of a whole group, but since cats tend to groom their heads and faces regularly with saliva-wetted paws, as well as licking those other parts of their bodies that they can reach, such a group smell is probably evanescent to the point of meaninglessness.

In addition to the glands on a cat's face, another set is found at the base of the tail. Veterinarians find that these glands often overproduce, creating a problem called stud-tail (a patch of hairlessness). In addition, a row of glands extends along the length of a tail, presumably used to mark something—as when your cat wraps its tail around your ankle.

Of course, any marking system that is so elaborate had to have evolved to accomplish something, and it clearly has to have something to do with the cat saying "I have been here." But whether it means "You are mine, dear," or "I want you to go away from here," or "I just want you to know that I have first dibs on the mice around here," remains to be determined. For now, the only feline scent-marking that has a perfectly well-understood effect is when females in heat or about to go into heat spray some urine around, the most potent of all attractants in the feline world.

Finally, in this olfactory picture, cats are (happily) known to bury their feces in the ground or the litter box, part of an overall cleanliness (compared with dogs, say) that recommends cats to many people. Indeed, so clean are cats generally that in the course of grooming themselves they will typically use up half of their daily water intake. Only certain tomcats—the real bigshots—leave their feces lying around in the open, clearly an advertisement. Other males who are less powerful (along with practically all females) will dutifully bury their feces in an apparent—but not proven—attempt to draw as little attention to themselves as possible.

The entire body of a cat is a communication device—its head, ears, eyes, expressions, postures, and movement—all bespeak the state of mind of a cat, whether it is angry, fearful, wants to fight, wants to avoid a fight, wants to approach another cat in a friendly way, wants another cat to go away. Just the way cats look at each other can convey something. If two cats stare at each other, a fight is very likely to ensue. On the other hand,

many people have watched two cats sitting in a field, say, still as rocks for long periods. They will look at each other when the other one is not looking, but look away when looked at. Some kind of contest is going on, a waiting game, until some signal that so far remains invisible to humans sends one or the other cat away. It would take an extraordinarily patient ethologist to figure out how this works.

Meanwhile much of a cat's body language is better understood, and a great deal of it suggests that a cat is a little furry bundle of barely repressed aggression. Most of the signals cats make with their posture, their tails, their ears, and their facial expressions are what scientists call distance-increasing signals—as opposed to distance-reducing signals that are more common among dogs and other highly social animals. For example, when a dog rolls over on its back, it may mean submission (especially to another dog), but when done for a human, it may only mean the dog wants its stomach scratched. When a cat rolls over on its back, it can expose four of its most dangerous weapons, its clawed feet, a posture that highly recommends departure by whomever is approaching. But a female cat rolls over on its back to encourage a swain or two, and kittens flop over on their side or back to initiate play. Context, context, context.

The position of the cat's tail can signal mood with considerable accuracy. If a cat arches its tail over its back, or carries the tail in an upside down *U*, or straight up, it is making a friendly approach and, if it is a kitten, it wants to play. Such an interest is also conveyed by eyes that are half closed and ears pointing forward. On the other hand, if a cat is about to be importuned by a more dominant one, it may simply crouch down and put its ears back flat, so as not to upset the intruder.

Cats have a variety of ways of silently suggesting that they want a minimum of social contact, and they rarely will strike out or fight without having provided a warning. One of the exceptions is when a cat encourages you to scratch its stomach but then, once it has had enough, gives you a swat, sometimes with claws arrayed. In this, as in public speaking, it is best to leave them wanting more. Many times humans and other species such as dogs fail to read a cat's warning signals, with painful results.

If the tip of a cat's tail or even the whole tail waves back and forth, it means the cat is uncomfortable with the situation at hand. If then the hair around the nape rises, followed by the hair down the length of the back, and the head is carried forward, as are the whiskers, it means the cat is about to attack. Signals that mean it is okay to come close—like the tail held as an inverted *U*—will mean just the reverse if the cat also raises its hackles. If the tail is arched over the back and the hackles are raised, it is a defensive posture, and the cat is likely to use this signal as it flees. The classic Hallowe'en cat—standing sideways, back arched, hair up, tail straight up, accompanied by hissing and spitting—is probably the ultimate defensive posture, one that has made many a dog, even very large ones, pause and reconsider its actions.

In general, it pays to be wary even of a typically friendly pet cat if its ears are flattened back on its head, its tail is wagging, or if it turns sideways and arches its back. This signals it is either a bit fearful or a bit angry, and it is best to leave it alone. Teaching children these signals is strongly advised.

Is all this domestic cat behavior simply carried over from its wild ancestor, the African wild cat, which is what you might

call an obligate loner, socializing with other cats only to mate or raise kittens? Or has the relatively short period—some four or more thousand years—since cats were domesticated led to some bits of nonwild behavior? Have some body language signals, for example, altered their meaning to accommodate the new more social situation that a house cat faces—including people, other cats, and even dogs? The answer is: not much. These two questions were investigated by John Bradshaw and Charlotte Cameron-Beaumont of the University of Southampton in England, and they found a couple of telling instances. First is the behavior called Tail Up, which is when a cat holds its tail stiff and fully erect—that is, straight up. All wild felids—from tigers to the smallest wild cats—do this when they are spraying urine. Kittens are also likely to do it when their mother is licking their ano-genital area. No wild felids raise their tails in this manner at any other time, as far as is known. But domestic cats will raise their tail in this manner not only when spraying but when making what they hope to convey is a friendly approach. Actually no one has made a detailed study of the behavior of the African wild cat, so we cannot totally rule out this tail-raising behavior as totally nonwild. But for now, anyway, it seems that using Tail Up as an affiliative signal is unique to domestic cats and may well be a specific adaptation to a more densely populated, more social life.

Similarly, wild felid kittens knead their mother's stomach near her teats when trying to feed and miaow, but do not do this as adults. But domesticated cats will knead their human companions and miaow at them when adults. In other words, domesticated cats have managed to hold on to these juvenile behaviors into adult life as a way perhaps of cementing relationships with humans. Holding the tail erect and miaowing and kneading would seem to be the only behaviors that have changed from the wild to help domestic cats signal their accommodation to life with humans. That hardly seems like a very long road to have traveled and, indeed, it reminds us of the suggestion of the British chronicler of domesticated animals, Juliet Clutton-Brock, that cats are not really domesticated animals but "exploiting captives."

In any event, and whatever wording one uses to describe the domestic cat, what seems most remarkable is that an animal that retains so much of its wild behavior, so much of its wild psychology, and such a preponderance of distance-increasing signals, has become such an accommodating, relatively patient, and even an affectionate member of human households.

RUDOLPH'S SON, HALF PERSIAN, INHERITED HIS FATHER'S LASSITUDE.

Chapter 10
The Association of Cats

The cat of the slums and alleys, starved, outcast, harried
. . . still displays the self-reliant watchfulness which man
has never taught it to lay aside.

—SAKI

*A*t the outset of the writing of this book I confidently produced a table of contents to impress my publisher with my overall command of the subject. Some of this table of contents has remained more or less intact, but in learning what has been discovered about the natural history of cats in recent decades, I have quietly made a number of changes.

For example, I originally had a chapter, falling about here, bravely called Cat Society. Possibly I had in mind, at some subconscious level, the musical comedy based on T. S. Eliot's book *Old Possum's Book of Practical Cats*. The musical, its title shortened simply to *Cats*, is about a colony of urban cats, feral cats living a slightly murky existence in the interstices of human civilization—that is, back alleys. It is joyous, sad, funny, moving, sophisticated, and utterly sensuous. In the lithe movements of the dancers, one might say it is exactly catlike. The music stays with one for weeks, playing itself over and over silently in one's brain, unforgettable and unavoidable—in all, a wonderful

work of art. It is also not a very realistic portrait of the society of urban cats.

We have what might be the makings of a feral cat congregation here on and around my two acres of land. There are an orange cat, a black-and-white one, and a gray one whom we often see patrolling our property and the neighborhood. A black one also lives in a ramshackle barn that needs restoring someday though that is probably one of those items on the dream list that homeowners tend to generate. Whenever the black cat leaves the barn, some jays begin screaming and follow it into the next pasture. Given that kind of hassle, we procrastinate by saying we don't want to disturb the black cat further by trying to fix up its barn.

Only in one circumstance have we seen any of these cats in a group. Most of the time and in all seasons but winter they appear and disappear singly. In the winter, however, Susanne is not going to let any animal go hungry just because it is cold outside and sometimes snowy. She feeds the cats on a table inside the open window of an old farm shed, and we can tell from footprints in the snow that it's cats and not raccoons who are attracted to the wet, meaty cat food Susanne puts out. She will often find at least three of the locals gathered, and they move away as she appears. The orange cat (rating high in boldness?) moves off a short distance, and the other two go farther off. Everyone sits and watches as Susanne comes and goes. And they remain there seated and still for a few minutes before heading for the shed. Why they wait is anybody's guess. By now they know she's not coming back. It's a cat thing, we say.

This hardly sounds like what anyone would call a society and, indeed, it would seem a bit overblown to talk of cat "society" when we have just spent a good deal of a chapter explaining that most of a cat's techniques of communication is given over to the avoidance of feline society. Social animals—like wolves, dolphins, and dogs—actively seek out company of their own kind and clearly depend upon one another in many ways. Cats, it seems, can take it or leave it. The word "society" often carries a connotation of a cooperative arrangement of members engaged in various activities, many of them communal. Ranking of members is often implied though not always the case.

What do the more sociable of wild cats tell us? All true society is widely thought to begin and revolve around the mother-offspring group. The loose associations of male cheetahs, up to four at a time, could hardly be called a society—it seems little more than a few drifters out on the road. Lions have a real society: a pride made up chiefly of females, a particular type of society called a matriarchy, with the matriarch's daughters and granddaughters making up most of the group. Often a few non-related males hang around on the fringes and, as noted earlier, freeload as often as not on the hunting efforts of the lionesses. The males may play a defensive role, trying to keep other males at bay (though this seems more self-interested than communal on their part). Young males (such as brothers) may leave the pride together, looking for another to infiltrate.

Of course, reports exist of real loners—one might even say obligate loners like mountain lions or tigers—seen sharing a carcass, but this is presumably a mother and yearling offspring. In such instances, the offspring are soon to depart for the solo life. And the young of all cat species tend to be social, even friendly with each other, playing and hunting together, until it is time to go off on their own. And, of course, females can be considered quite social, spending the better part of each year in the company of their kittens. But the mother-offspring bond,

while it is the cornerstone of society, is not exactly the complex structure that "society" typically implies.

Where then do domestic cats stand in all of this? To begin with, all the other animals that humans have brought under their sway—from dogs and goats and pigs and horses to such near-domesticates as Asian elephants or llamas—are distinctly social animals and always were so in the wild, living in packs or herds. Cats are the only domestic animals that derive from loners in the wild. The notion of herding cats is a colorful way of describing anarchy.

As Stephen Budiansky has written, domestic cats "do show one very dramatic behavioral change even from African wildcats, in that they will tolerate living in social groups, and even form them on their own." The key word here would seem to be "tolerate." In other words, there are situations in which for one reason or another domestic cats will put up with the company of others. And there are instances—no one knows how common this is—when feline members of a human household, and especially littermates, will develop what can only be called friendships: lasting, close relationships that include even joint hunting, that most private of cat activities. On the other hand, as most cat owners know all too well, it can take a lot of patience to introduce a new cat into a household where other cats have already made themselves at home. Books written for veterinarians usually supply a good deal of advice on overcoming the "distance producing" behavior that will (with effort and luck) discombobulate one's peaceable kingdom for only a short while.

Where something approaching the complexity of a society exists among cats is among groups of feral cats—those found in cities like T. S. Eliot's, and farm cats. These differ from stray cats that have left human homes and remain alone, existing primarily if not totally by solo hunting of wild prey. What passes for cat society occurs when a group of feral cats live near a constant source of food—such as a garbage dump, or a carelessly managed restaurant Dumpster, or other conglomerations of unwanted human food. These are typically cats that for a few generations have lived in groups outside of human homes. Many such feral groups are sustained by sympathetic humans who feed them but who make little or no effort to redomesticate them. Redomesticating feral cats is about as rewarding as trying to herd them, and most people who try it soon find something else to do.

By going online, one can look over the shoulders of many amateur feral cat colony watchers who report on the comings and goings of the cats in greater or lesser detail. Perhaps the most detailed and longest scientific study of feral cats to date has been undertaken by David W. Macdonald and his associates, Nobuyuki Yamaguchi and Gillian Kerby, at the University of Oxford. They put in some 3,000 hours of close observations of three separate feral farm-cat colonies: a small one (four to nine adult members), medium (seven to eleven), and large (sixteen to twenty-five). In all, they recorded some 63,000 cat interactions, and 59,000 measurements of the distances the cats maintained between each other at various times. Each colony, regardless of size, was made up of females of more than one "lineage," meaning basically mothers and daughters (and in some cases, granddaughters) with one or more unrelated tomcats hanging around.

In each case, there were "central lineages," meaning a related group of females who stayed closest to the source of food—let us call it a restaurant Dumpster. Farther off were "peripheral lineages," usually smaller in number and, not surprisingly, less

well fed and with less reproductive success. Access to the Dumpster was largely universal but not equal. When there were several tomcats associated with a group, these adult males fought among themselves and were aggressive toward the females. If there were one tom and several juvenile males, the tom would fight the youngsters, prolonging their juvenile period. Females, however, rarely showed much by way of antagonism to the toms (except for the highly edgy behavior during mating).

The main measure of how closely affiliated female cats were was how close they would sit to one another. Cats from a given lineage would rest some ten to fifteen feet from one another or closer. Cats from different lineages would typically stay some twenty to thirty feet apart. In each lineage, one female seemed to be the boss, and when such a cat died, her place was taken up by another female from the lineage who might (and in some instances did) force some members of her group into a more peripheral existence.

Most of these findings suggest that group living among feral cats has a bit of a way to go to become anything like a peaceable queendom, but there is an area of considerable cooperation: the suckling and raising of kittens. Females originally from the same litter will often share the responsibility for a sister's kittens, from suckling them and bringing solid food, but even to a kind of midwifery, licking the mother's genital area and grooming the kittens at birth. (Adult females were also seen grooming other females, though briefly.)

The child-rearing cooperation is typically reciprocal among sisters, but its emotional hold on these helpful aunts seems to end at some point during the kittens' growth into juveniles. The mother cats soon pay no more attention to their nieces and nephews than they do to any other bunch of young cats.

Recently an Italian study of a feral cat colony showed that the toms, rather than go to the food source ahead of the others, dominating it, backed away to let the females eat first. And the females appeared to let the kittens eat ahead of them. This all sounds counterintuitive until one gives the toms the wisdom to put the impregnated females onto the chow line first, since it is best if the unborn kittens (and the live ones), all carrying the males' genes, get plenty to eat. How widespread this kind of evolutionary altruism is remains unknown. The Italian colony could be unique.

The fact is, there isn't all that much to cat society. Of course, there are surely signals among them that go unnoticed even by the closest human observers. Also there are advantages to being in a group under the right circumstances that are not altogether clear. For example, biologists have wondered if lions gather in prides of various sizes because it provides a more certain share of the food available for each lion, or because over time evolution has created a situation in which predators and prey tend to keep both populations at fairly steady levels, damping any tendency to boom-and-bust cycles like the legendary population explosion of arctic hares, followed by rapid growth of arctic foxes, followed by a crash in hare numbers and then in fox numbers, and so on ad infinitum.

Forming such groups does not appear to be something that cats do by way of the unalterable commands of their genes; indeed, most cats resist it. The case can be made that it is something that each generation of each lineage out there around the Dumpster learns from its elders. For better or worse (and feral cats' lives are indeed hard), group living may be a cultural affair when it comes to cats.

RUDOLPH, THE LAID-BACK PERSIAN, IN 1967.

Chapter 11
Breeds, Individuals, and Friends

There are no ordinary cats.

—COLETTE

We are talking about personality here. It is hard to make scientific statements about the personality of cats (or humans for that matter) because personality is a concept that is really resistant to formulas, numbers, statistics, quantification. So most experimental scientists will simply avoid the topic altogether, although they may own cats themselves and may also describe their cats (in nonscientific terms) as having certain personality traits, such as timidity or the opposite. In fact, every cat owner recognizes his or her cat's distinct personality, but it is a subject that admits of few broad generalizations. Psychologists have tried to pin down the features that go into creating a personality (or temperament) in animals, and we will look at some of these efforts a bit later. First we take a look at breeds.

People who breed cats for show purposes or just for sale to breed aficionados will tell you about their breed's personality

traits, and sometimes veterinarians and others will confirm (or, rarely, contradict) such commentary. Breeding cats to certain specifications is, for the most part, a fairly recent phenomenon compared with the ancient breeding of dogs or horses for particular kinds of work, or breeding dogs for particular appearances mandated for dog shows that became popular in the nineteenth century. Only a tiny percentage—less than 5 percent—of the eighty million cats in the United States are particular breeds, and few of these breeds go back before the turn of the twentieth century. Siamese and some other Asian-style breeds may be quite old. The rest—more than 95 percent of U.S. cats—are just cats: tabbies for the most part, who look pretty much like their wild ancestor, the African wild cat. But we have learned that breeding animals for one or two aesthetic traits will, before long, bring about other consequences that are usually unforeseen, including personality traits. And breeding for a personality trait like boldness can bring about unplanned physical changes.

Domestic cat breeds are fewer than dog breeds, and the differences between cat breeds far smaller than among dogs. Most cat breeds are about the same size. The Maine Coon cat and the Savannah cat, a very recent breed we mentioned before (domestic cat plus serval), are among the larger cat breeds, but there simply is no feline equivalent to the huge difference between a 180-pound mastiff and an accessory Chihuahua that fits in a lady's purse. (Some idiot has apparently bred a Chihuahua that weighs four ounces! This seems to me as pointless as breeding a mouse-sized cat.) Thank heavens that—for now at least—no pet cat of any known breed is big enough to make a normal nonallergic person physically uncomfortable if it sits in one's lap, or small enough to be carried around in a change purse.

My personal view is that breeding animals for extreme characteristics such as hairlessness or freakishly big ears or oddly shaped heads is manic human behavior carried out for reasons that have little or nothing to do with the welfare of the animal in question. The more a breed of cat looks like a regular cat (such as the African wild cat) the better, as far as I am concerned, even though I recognize that my view is a narrow one. One reason for this view is that the excessive inbreeding typically practiced to establish breeds almost always leads eventually to unforeseen disabilities, ailments, and diseases. In the case of dogs, among some 350 breeds, only a handful of recently created ones like Australian shepherds are not given to particular health conditions. The situation is less severe among cats, as shown in Appendix B in this book, but it remains a threat, especially in the hands of overly enthusiastic and careless breeders. Evolution takes place, after all, at a relatively stately pace, and hastening the process by artificial selection is best done with great care and knowledge.

With all of that, cat breeds are seen to have what at least are personality *tendencies*, mostly benign. Siamese are well known to be highly vocal and fussy about many matters. Persians are widely perceived as phlegmatic. Many writers on the subject, including veterinarians, have listed personalities by breed and some of their findings for breeds common in America are summarized here.

To begin with, for most personality traits, Siamese and Persian cats are on opposite ends of the spectrum. Siamese cats (and other oriental short-haired cats like Burmese and Abyssinians) have been called the most vocal, active, and destructive; least friendly to other cats; most intolerant of handling; excit-

able; and playful. In other words, if you want to live with what might be called a whole lot of action, get one or two of these. On the other hand, Persians (and some other long-haired cats) demand the least attention, give the least overt affection, are most inactive, least destructive, least vocal, among the calmest, least playful, and least hygienic. (On the other hand, another study showed Persians to be cleaner than Siamese.)

Our orange Persian male, Rudolph, had a brother who had won the national championship as best in show at Madison Square Garden, but Rudolph was essentially a placid barn cat, exemplifying virtually all the personality traits listed above for Persians. He mainly just lay around watching the world go by, happy to be played with briefly by any of a houseful of daughters, but also quite content to be ignored. Rudolph was, in fact, the most phlegmatic mammal I have ever known; I have seen bearded dragons (a largish sort of lizard from Australia) who are more active. In a household the personality of which was generally a bit chaotic, Rudolph—unflappable and easy to please—was probably the perfect cat. Some neighbors who lived on the other side of our back alley took to feeding him treats, so he began to put in some time at their house daily. Then these neighbors (the family of an Episcopalian priest) announced their plan to move to a distant state, and said they intended to take Rudolph with them. We protested, of course. Rudolph was our cat and had been for more than a decade. But in what we could only think of as a highly unpriestly maneuver, they absconded with Rudolph, our perfect city-teen house cat. This was a sneaky sort of thing, like the way the Baltimore Colts football team was spirited off to Indianapolis in the middle of the night. Short of filing a criminal complaint and looking into the legal thickets of cat extradition, we could only hope that the move did not upset Rudolph's remarkable equanimity. He had been very much at home in the back alley, and cats don't appreciate moving.

Earlier, Susanne had a half-Siamese that talked incessantly and bonded with a baby raccoon she rescued from a pet store. The two were inseparable until the cat, named Gordouli after a song favored by Balliol College at Oxford, was run over in the street, and the raccoon, called Coon Laude, returned to the wild. Normally (and here where we live now), raccoons wage predatory war on the local cats. One rule in natural affairs is that practically all rules have exceptions. Recall, for example, the cat Cosmo suckling the dog Mona. This is, I think, a good thing. It keeps you on your toes.

If you look through the various cat fancier magazines, you will find a great number of adjectives coupled to breeds, adjectives that all sound pretty much alike: good-natured, tolerant, friendly, gentle, affable, even-tempered, ultra-affectionate, equable, calm, relaxed. A few standouts are the "languorous" Cameo Longhair, the "loyal" Black Longhair, the "civilized" Birman, the "shy" Russian Blue, and the Egyptian Mau that is "good at learning tricks, enjoys walking on a lead."

If you want to have more than one cat in your house, and you insist on having only distinct cat breeds, get yourself Domestic Shorthairs. They seem to be the friendliest to other cats. In this desirable characteristic as in several others, it turns out that neutered males can be the best bet, according to an elaborate study by the British veterinarian Bruce Fogle. There is plenty of information available online, in cat magazines, and of course from breeders, on the temperament of the many breeds available today, much of it improving if taken with a bit of salt.

Evidence exists that merely the color of a cat carries with it certain personality traits. One study showed that non-agouti cats, especially black cats, are more tolerant of the crowded conditions of living in a city apartment. (My long-ago black cat, Cat, lived in a residential part of Washington, D.C., for most of his life and seemed perfectly at ease, but I don't know that he would have enjoyed life half as much if he had not been able to go outside on his own and prowl. He was enough of a city kid not to get run over.) Red, cream, and tortoiseshell Shorthair kittens evidently make more escape attempts when handled by humans than other colors. Male cats with orange in their coats seem to be more aggressive than males without orange. The reason why orange toms are rare, especially in cities, is that aggressive tomcats (as we saw in Chapter 5 on territory and reproduction) tend to fight each other, while less aggressive males slip in and mate with the female in estrus. So orange males have less success in mating for all their macho—at least in cities. Orange toms make out better in the country since the overall density of toms is less, so a given tom will spend less time fighting and more time charming the local females.

Blue-eyed white cats, and to a lesser extent orange-eyed white cats, tend to deafness, as do some cats that are merely white-spotted (if the spots reach the ears). Such cats often suffer an irreversible degeneration of the inner ear that begins a few days after birth. Why? Probably the genes that control the color of coats lie close to genes governing the function of the nervous system, but this will all come out in the ongoing analysis of the cat genome possible now that its 20,285 genes have been sequenced thanks to Cinnamon, the four-year-old Abyssinian cat in Maryland in 2006. Having this blueprint, among others including humans, dogs, and mice, is promised to bring about various medical revolutions; no doubt it will. In the meantime, there seem to be some whimsical researchers out there, such as the Korean group who in 2007 successfully transferred certain genes to a cat that cause it to glow in the dark if subjected to infrared. Certainly this would not be a helpful trait to a cat hunting mice in the dark. However, the Korean whimsy was not to be outdone. The announcement of the glow-in-the-dark cat was followed in a matter of days by the announcement that Japanese researchers had replaced a gene dedicated to fear and produced a mouse that is not afraid of cats.

The alert reader will have noticed back there that when one study showed that Persians tend to the unhygienic, another showed them to lead in hygiene. Both studies could be right, depending on which Persian cats were being studied. A great deal of individual personality variation exists *within* cat breeds, probably more than exists *between* cat breeds. Just as with dogs, you can have extremely alert individuals in a phlegmatic breed and lazy individuals among the members of an energetic breed. A breeding program designed to produce cats who are highly friendly to humans can turn up individuals who are timid and unfriendly. It is not all a matter of genes. Genes provide an animal (or a plant, for that matter) with a range of possibilities waiting to be expressed at the proper time. But the timing of their expression, and even the intensity with which they are expressed, can vary quite a bit, leading to minor or major variations both in anatomy and psychology.

A lot of the variation in gene expression depends on what happens in the cat's environment, and a cat's environment in-

cludes a host of influences ranging from parental care, nutrition, the activities of littermates, and the presence of other adult
cats (as in feral colonies) to the properly or improperly timed
presence of humans among kittens, and other factors, some of
which no doubt remain to be found. Being raised in a world of
horizontal or vertical stripes can affect how a kitten will see the
world for the rest of its life. Since these environmental effects
are going to be different, however slightly, for every kitten in a
litter, it stands to reason that every cat is going to have a unique
personality. Looking into the personalities of individual cats (or
other animals) is a great challenge for scientists.

The scientific method for figuring out if cats like each other,
for example, is to make exhaustingly long and numerous observations of how closely (in meters) two cats will sit and for how
long at a time, measured over and over and over, and compared
with similar observations of other cats. Indiana Jones types
need not apply. This is slow and painstaking work. Similarly,
it has taken weeks, even months, of observation, monitoring
a list of traits, to begin to learn how cats develop recognizably
individual personalities.

One early observation was that kittens sired by toms who
were themselves friendly to humans were likely to become
friendly to humans. Since kittens practically never see their fathers, friendliness appeared to be genetic and based on paternity.
On the other hand, other studies showed that kittens who were
handled by people during their sensitive period (from three to
about eight weeks) were also inclined to be friendly to humans.
Scientists were able to discover that there was an optimum
amount of handling that produced the best results—some forty
minutes to an hour each day, especially by one handler. Most

kittens, however, could generalize the experience of one human handler to several and be just as friendly. Handling the kitten for more than an hour a day produced no significant additional friendliness. And cats—most of them, at any rate—are known to grow intolerant of handling after a while, the amount of time varying from cat to cat, of course.

Meanwhile, if the mother alone raised a kitten, it would not usually turn out to be particularly friendly to humans. But if the mother raised it with another kitten, friendliness was increased. The best option was for the mother to raise a litter larger than two. So here we have at least three factors involved in making a kitten friendly to humans. How to sort them out?

To begin with, genes do not code for specific behaviors, so the paternity influence is genetic but indirect. It was found, for instance, that kittens sired by human-friendly fathers were also more likely to approach a new object or situation quickly rather than hanging back. So the father's role seemed to be to produce a characteristic of overall boldness in the kittens, and this would also serve to put the kittens in close touch with humans in very short order.

By controlling matters experimentally, scientists sorted out the factors with some precision. At one year of age, kittens with human-friendly fathers, and who had been properly handled by humans in early life, were quicker to approach people and spent more time with them. Kittens who were handled but had a human-unfriendly father, and kittens with a human-friendly father but who went unhandled, were noticeably less friendly to humans at one year of age. Least friendly overall were kittens with a human-unfriendly father, who also went unhandled.

The questions to ask a breeder of cats—be they purebreds or

just good old house cats—should be pretty clear from all this, though there are no guarantees. To throw another variable into the mix, some observers have found that the friendly effects deriving from paternity (that is, genes) can show up at various times in different situations, sometimes postponed for as much as a year. This inconsistency across time may be a result of the overall development of the kitten and the multiple timings of various genetically determined traits and actions.

Much of the same can be seen in the development of predatory proficiency in kittens. At two or three months, kittens will show a wide range of proficiency. By six months, however, most kittens (but not all) show the same ability to catch prey. It gets more complex than that, too. For example, if a kitten is given a single kind of prey to hunt, it will become proficient at that, but many kittens will not be able to generalize that ability to other prey species.

Various traits have been found to be fairly consistent throughout a cat's life. Inquisitive kittens are likely to remain that way as adults. The same with boldness (not easily distinguished from inquisitiveness, one would think) and activeness, and a high frequency of rubbing. Timid and/or nervous kittens will almost surely remain that way. All of this presupposes that life is relatively steady and nice. But if a family member of a well-socialized and friendly cat abuses it, it may never be friendly to family members again, though it may (for some reason) remain friendly to human strangers. Or it may give up on people altogether and, if able, disappear into the world of the feral. Cats and dogs (and horses) seem to have long memories, especially for things that were scary or otherwise unpleasant.

And what cats may decide is unpleasant can become bizarre

individual tics, and how they arise is baffling. For example, a neighbor of ours named Sally (yet another one) has an eighteen-year-old cat named Sallyann who was perfectly happy when her Grammy-winning Dobro-playing owner practiced or played in the house. But she detested any and all other live music. One week when Sally was gone on a gig, the young man who was renting space in the basement came upstairs and began playing his guitar. The cat simply left, disappeared. This was in the dead of winter, freezing temperatures and deep snow around the house. The woebegone house sitter and the neighbors assumed after a few days that the cat was surely dead: they had even seen the tracks of a mountain lion near the house. Everyone grieved the loss of Sally's cat, but when she came home after several days, the cat emerged from under the porch where she had somehow managed to survive without food or water. Sally fed her up and she was fine, but she continued to detest music played by others. Overwrought, perhaps? A bit melodramatic to say the least—not unlike a teenager or an opera diva. But every inch an individual, and utterly devoted to her Sally and all her works.

It should come as little surprise that the most rigorous analysis of the individual style or temperament of domestic cats has concerned itself mostly with the degree of friendliness with which cats embrace humans. Humans want to know about this aspect of cat behavior probably more than any other. It is also the cat's most astounding feature, when you think about it.

Here is an animal whose direct ancestor only a few thousand years ago was a lone hunter, a soloist for life, most of whose behavior, vocalizations, and body language are geared to keep-

ing other cats at a distance if not altogether out of the picture. Here is no herd animal, no creature drawn to the life of the pack, like dogs or cows or elephants or dolphins or horses. Here is the lone stalker, an animal so preoccupied with itself that it will spend up to a third of its waking hours licking its own fur. And this animal, if treated well, will allow itself to find warmth and affection, food (at least some), and *companionship* with you and me. This is an astonishing turnabout, however only partly achieved (if you need to make comparisons with dogs, which most cat owners do not need to do).

How is such a major psychological turnabout possible? Poets and philosophers and others have tried to explain this, usually with reference to the nature of the cat itself. But we are talking about a two-way street here. Why would cats put up with humans? Are we not the alpha creatures in this equation? In fact, the alpha male–alpha female stuff hardly seems to apply to cat-human arrangements. One of the best, if least romantic, explanations for cats tolerating and even liking humans comes from the scientists who have made all those endless observations and measurements. The answer lies not in the suggestion that cats, once they were partly domesticated, have become more like us. It lies in the obvious fact that we humans are *nothing at all like cats.* We do not compete with cats for food or mates. We do not attempt to usurp a cat's space. We do not go to great lengths to pester cats, training them to do various jobs of work for us, like pulling little carts or helping us run down deer or fetching dead birds out of the water or plastic disks out of the air, or even babysitting for our children. Indeed, if we are smart, we just let cats be cats, and recognize that they have done a pretty good job of domesticating us.

The Wild Cats of the World

We can only hope that the increased awareness of the problems that face our environment and the need to do something now rather than later will also benefit the plight of the most specialized predators the world has ever seen.

—ANDREW KITCHENER, AUTHOR OF
The Natural History of Wild Cats

Only sixty Asian cheetahs exist now (at the beginning of 2008) and only about 450 Siberian tigers. Of the thirty-six species of wild cat, only a handful are considered safely situated on the planet. The mountain lions of the Americas are probably the least threatened big cat in the world, being adaptable to differing environmental conditions, and inhabiting much of the North American West as well as some northern parts of Central and South America. Some subspecies of the mountain lion (or cougar, among its many names), like the Florida panther, are probably doomed, but the Florida panther has been bred with the Texas version and so isn't truly itself anymore.

The range of jaguars is similarly large on paper, extending from the Mexican–U.S. border into Argentina. But it is in separate patches, and there is no coordinated international plan to create sufficient refuges (and satisfactory corridors between

them). African lions may be in pretty good shape in terms of their potential to survive, but their numbers now are less than half of what they were only a few generations ago.

Most of the threat today comes from loss of habitat—with rain forests, savannahs, and other ecosystems being given over to agriculture and livestock to feed the increasingly urban human race. It has been estimated that about half of the photo-synthesis that goes on on the surface of the earth is now given over to agriculture, leaving about half to create habitat for wild animals. Some 80 percent of all large-mammal species have seen their habitat reduced in this century. Around the world, fresh water—now being directed to urban concentrations—is the limiting factor of the future for virtually all human enter-prises, including the setting aside of refuges for wildlife.

Some of the threat, as with the tigers, comes from bizarre cultural beliefs about the increase available in health or manli-ness from the use of tiger parts. And, of course, poachers and smugglers go for illegal profits even in areas that have been set aside specifically for these remarkable animals and their prey species and, thereby, chunks of their entire ecosystem. Such set-asides are the only hope for most of the big cats; many spe-cies of the smaller cats have recently achieved such champion-ing, but the poaching goes on—in the hundreds of thousands of wild cats each year, it is estimated.

The African (or Egyptian or Near Eastern) wild cat that gave rise to the domestic cat is in danger of extinction, ironically, by inbreeding with feral domestic cats. Similarly, the Scottish wild cat, the last remnant of the European version, could also wind up as a forgotten genetic component of the feral domestic cat population. And so, Kurt Vonnegut said, it goes.

The largely unpredictable effects of unprecedentedly rapid global climate change currently gathering steam (as it were) is bound to have profound effects on local ecosystems and wildlife. For example, the Pantanal, a vast region of swamps and rivers in South America, is home to about one-fourth of the hemisphere's jaguars. Where will they go, and how, if those waters begin to dry up? Similarly, the Sunderbans, a huge region of sea girt marshlands on the India-Bangladesh border, is home to a considerable fraction of the world's tigers. It could vanish under the floodwaters of the Indian Ocean by the end of this century, if not before, as sea levels rise around the world.

It is a sorry litany, to be sure. Wildlife managers and zoos will do their best to maintain some of the genes of these most specialized predators the world has ever seen, but where will international, national, local, and even personal priorities lie in the coming century in a world with some nine billion humans vying for resources? No one knows. Here, for the record, is a brief catalogue (pun not intended but noted) of the wild felines of the only planet in the universe where such creatures are known to exist.

Biologists break up the cats of the world into four groups or lineages—the Ocelot lineage, the Domestic Cat lineage, the Pantherine lineage (which includes the cougar and the cheetah and the serval), and the Panthera group (which includes lynxes and all the other big cats).

Ocelot Lineage

Ocelot (*Felis pardalis*): The best-known South American medium-sized cat, it has been kept as a pet, and some of the pet

ocelots have been loosed in Florida where they might establish a self-sustaining population. It lives in a variety of habitats from rain forest to semideserts, marshland and riverbanks, but not in open country.

Margay (*Felis wiedii*): Smaller and more blotchily spotted than the ocelot, the margay has uniquely flexible ankles that permit it to be comfortably arboreal. Its range is similar to that of the ocelot except that it is now extinct in the United States.

Tiger Cat (*Felis tigrina*): Like the margay in marking and range (in which it is rare), it is one of the smallest South American cats. It has a shorter tail than the margay, suggesting it is less arboreal. Melanistic (black) ones have been seen in southeastern Brazil. Also called the little spotted cat and the oncilla.

Geoffroy's Cat (*Felis geoffroy*): A small cat with a ground color ranging from ocher to gray, with small black spots, this cat has suffered from the fur trade since the use of ocelots and margays for this purpose declined. A frequenter of scrubby forests and plains in foothills up to about 9,000 feet, its range is limited to Argentina, Uruguay, and Bolivia.

Kodkod (*Felis guigna*): South America's smallest cat resembles Geoffroy's cat but with a ringed tail. Like Geoffroy's, it has black ears with white spots on the back. Found in forests in Chile, not much else is known about it.

Pampas Cat (*Felis colocolo*): Resembling the European wild cat with highly variable coat color and gray ears, it lives in habitats that range from open grasslands to humid forest in most of southern South America.

Mountain Cat (*Felis jacobita*): Rare and little known, it has silver fur striped with brown or orange, dark gray ears, and a bushy tail with black rings. Restricted to arid parts of the Andes.

Domestic Cat Lineage

Wild Cat (*Felis silvestris*): Discussed in the text. With one of the greatest ranges for small cats, its markings vary considerably with habitat. Taxonomists argue whether the various types are all one species or, perhaps, three. Hybridization with the domestic cat to which it gave rise has now obscured relationships of the wild cat's subspecies, which include the African wild cat (*Felis silvestris lybica*), which is more gracile than the European, and the Indian Desert Cat (*Felis silvestris ornata*), which is sand colored with black spots and thought by some to be the progenitor of the Asian cat breeds.

Domestic Cat (*Felis catus* or *Felis silvestris catus*): Of which perhaps enough has been said herein.

Chinese Desert Cat (*Felis bieti*): Possibly another *silvestris*, it is almost unknown in detail. It is pale yellowish with a few stripes on it legs, and tufts of hair on its feet for crossing hot sand. Its range extends from the desert to the steppes and mountains of China and Mongolia.

Jungle Cat (*Felis chaus*): Much larger than *F. silvestris*, the Egyptians mummified many of them for ritual purposes. Pale in color with a few stripes on the legs and tufts of hair in the ears (like the Chinese Desert Cat), they are found not only in swampy grounds in Egypt but in woodlands, open plains, and croplands in India and southwestern Asia.

Sand Cat (*Felis margarita*): A desert cat found from the Sahara through the Middle East into Turkistan, it digs burrows to rest in during the day and hunts at night. Its markings are elaborate—a sandy ground coat with a reddish streak on its face and red-brown ears tipped with black. It has black rings on its tail with a black tip.

Black-footed Cat (*Felis nigripes*): Africa's version of the Sand Cat, it lives in deserts and grasslands. It has black spots on brown fur, cheek stripes, and bars on its legs. The bottoms of its feet are black (as are those of domestic cats and wild cats).

Pallas's Cat (*Felis manul*): Compact with long fur that varies from light gray to reddish, the tips of its hair is white. It has streaks on the side of its head, and rings on the tail. It looks "like a ball of fluff," according to Andrew Kitchener, and this serves to insulate it against the cold of the Russian deserts and rocky mountains. As noted in the text, its pupils remain round, while its eyes adjust to various light conditions.

Pantherine Lineage

Leopard Cat (*Felis bengalensis*): Very common throughout southern and eastern Asia, the Philippines, and Indonesia, it is the size of domestic cats, yellow with black spots like its namesake, though ground color and size vary with geography, with the Philippine version the smallest and the Manchurian version the largest. Its range includes virtually every terrestrial habitat.

Iriomote Cat (*Felis iriomotensis*): Discovered in the 1960s on a tiny island at the southern end of Japan's Ryukyu Islands, some hundred of these cats survive. Like a short-legged Leopard Cat (of which it may be a subspecies), it has a short tail and a long body with dark stripes on its neck.

Rusty-spotted Cat (*Felis rubiginosa*): One of the smallest of cats, its range is southern India, where it inhabits grasslands, and Sri Lanka, where it inhabits tropical forest.

Fishing Cat (*Felis viverrina*): Originally thought to be a civet, this robust cat is found throughout most of Asia. Its feet are slightly webbed, and its claws do not fully retract into their sheaths. It frequents mangrove swamps and marshy areas, and often enters the water to catch fish and frogs, which it catches in its mouth, unlike the way a domestic cat tries with its paws to lift your goldfish out of the tank.

Flat-headed Cat (*Felis planiceps*): Considered the world's oddest cat, it has a flattened head, a long body, and a short tail and legs. Brown with white spots underneath, its tail is yellow underneath. The flat head is thought to be an adaptation to fishing, something like an aquatic weasel. Its range is restricted to three Indonesian islands. Kitchener suggests that this cat is more deserving of the name Fishing Cat than *Felis viverrina*.

African Golden Cat (*Felis aurata*): It comes in a red phase (called golden) and a gray phase (called silver), and its spotting and other markings come in four distinct patterns from spotted all over to almost none. Usually found in the high rain forests of West, Central, and East Africa, it is a nocturnal hunter seen resting diurnally in the trees.

Temminck's Golden Cat (*Felis temminckii*): Larger than its look-alike, the Leopard Cat, it lives in wooded and rocky areas stretching from Malaya and Sumatra north to the Himalayas and China. It is heavily spotted in the north, less so in the south.

Bay Cat (*Felis badia*): It occurs only on Borneo, and in two color phases—brown with faint spots, and slate gray. In both the face is striped white. It is a creature of Borneo's tropical forests.

Serval (*Felis serval*): The unwitting progenitor of the Savannah cat breed, it is common throughout much of central and southern Africa in all habitats but tropical forests and des-

erts. Its long legs allow it to hunt in tall grass prairies where it pounces on its prey, which it hears with its exceptionally large ears. Its coat is typically yellow with black spots, the more boldly spotted ones living in drier areas.

Caracal (*Felis caracal*): With tufted ears that are black, its name derives from a Turkish word for black-ear. It is a robust version of the serval, reddish brown with a white eye-ring and a black line from the eye to the nose. Found in practically every habitat but rain forests from Africa north and south of the Sahara to India.

Puma (*Felis concolor*): Also known as the Cougar, Mountain Lion, Panther, Catamount, Mountain Screamer, and a host of other names including (Kitchener points out with an exclamation point) the Purple Feather. It ranges from Argentina to Canada, in a variety of habitats: mountain forests, lowland rain forests, grasslands, swamps, and, in winter when the cold forces it down from the mountains, my yard. The puma's cubs are spotted during their first weeks, an aid to concealment, but the adults are plain coated, ranging from reddish brown to gray. The puma is capable of speeds of forty-five miles an hour and of jumping eighteen feet into the air.

Jaguarundi (*Felis yagouaroundi*): Resembling an otter more than a cat, the Jaguarundi is active at dusk and dawn and is more diurnal than most other cats. Unmarked, they are found from the southern United States to Argentina, but they are rare in the north. A feral population lives in Florida, unlikely pets gone astray.

Cheetah (*Acinonyx jubatus*): Much discussed in the text of this book, the cheetah used to range from India to Africa, but its range is now greatly restricted outside of Asia, except for a handful of Asian cheetahs mentioned earlier in the appendix. At some point in their history, the African cheetahs went through a population bottleneck so limited that cheetahs are now virtually without any genetic variation, a situation discovered in the 1970s by researchers at the Smithsonian's National Zoological Park. This puts the entire population at risk if an epidemic of some sort strikes, and also makes breeding less easily accomplished both in the wild and, as a hedge against such an epidemic, in zoos.

Panthera Group

Eurasian Lynx (*Lynx lynx*): The largest of lynxes—a medium-sized group with short tails and tufted ears, specialized as rabbit hunters—it is widely distributed in northern and central Asia with a few small populations in Europe. Like the other lynxes, it has large paws for moving across snow. The European Lynx is typically an inhabitant of high forests, but the Spanish subspecies frequents even old sand dunes.

Canada Lynx (*Lynx canadensis*): Smaller than the European species, with white-tipped fur, it is barely spotted. It occurs throughout Canada and the northern United States, and has been introduced as far south as Colorado. There are various color varieties including a rare blue one.

Bobcat (*Lynx rufus*): The smallest lynx, it has a short tail with black rings, and it ranges from tan to brown with dark stripes. It inhabits the United States and Mexico in pine forests, mountains, and semideserts. Its diet extends beyond the rabbits and hares taken by its larger cousins.

Clouded Leopard (*Neofelis nebulosa*): Highly arboreal with

a long bushy tail for balance and flexible ankles for climbing (and descending), the Clouded Leopard is a creature of the rain forests of Indonesia, southeastern Asia, and China. Pale with blotchy (cloudlike) markings, it is recently extinct in Taiwan. Black (melanistic) versions have been seen in Borneo.

Marbled Cat (*Pardofelis marmorata*): Another arboreal species with a long bushy tail, this is a miniature version of the Clouded Leopard with similar markings. Extremely rare, it is found in tropical forests from Nepal to Borneo and Sumatra where it is believed to hunt prey in the trees. Like other cats of the tropical forests of the world, it is threatened with habitat loss, perhaps more severely than the others because of its natural rarity.

Snow Leopard (*Panthera uncia*): A central Asian cat of the mountains, it uses its thick tail to wrap around itself for warmth. In summer it inhabits alpine meadows and rocky highlands up to 18,000 feet, and follows its prey down to the lowlands in winter. Gray and white, below, it has dark spots and rosettes. Rarely seen, it is particularly threatened by hunting and loss of prey.

Tiger (*Panthera tigris*): The largest and probably most familiar of all the big cats. There were eight subspecies (based on geography) but three—Caspian, Javan, and Balinese—are already extinct. All the others are deeply threatened. The Russians have recently established a huge refuge for the Siberian tiger, following the lead of several other Asian nations. The largest occur in Siberia; the smallest in Indonesia.

Leopard (*Panthera pardus*): Pale with dark rosettes and spots, the leopard is found in virtually every terrestrial habitat in Asia and Africa, from tropical rain forests to deserts, and from sea level to some 15,000 feet in elevation. The most widespread of big cats, scientists count fifteen subspecies, all based on geography.

Jaguar (*Panthera onca*): Recently seen in the southwestern United States, the jaguar is found all the way south to Argentina, but has been eliminated from many parts of its former range. Unlike the leopard's rosettes, the jaguar has spots within the rosettes; also, the jaguar is a stockier cat than the leopard, its tail and legs being shorter. It is an animal of forests and savannahs, as well as deserts (even though it prefers to live near water). Like the tiger, it is a good swimmer.

Lion (*Panthera leo*): This is the most social of the wild cats, as discussed in the text, and the only cat in which the male differs considerably from the female in appearance, the male having a mane that ranges from dark brown to tan.

Both sexes have a tuft at the tip of their tails, and they are without markings as adults. The cubs have spots, an aid to concealment. Their natural range was from Africa and Europe to India, but they are now confined mostly to parks and refuges in Africa along with a small population in India's Gir forest.

APPENDIX B

Cat Food Alert

One crucially important feature of the feline life that should be clear as a bell now is that all cats in the wild subsist almost entirely on other animals. Or as California veterinarian Lisa A. Pierson says, "You would never see a wild cat chasing down a herd of biscuits on the plains of Africa." The fact that domestic cats, like all other members of the cat family, are obligate carnivores means, among other things, that a responsible cat owner is *obligated* to provide it with real meat protein. A growing number of veterinarians and cat nutritionists have taken this to heart, imploring cat owners to provide their pet cats with a quality canned food diet rather than dry kibble. On the other hand, many vets and their technical aides have not been trained in nutritional science, and take nutritional advice for cats from the cat food manufacturers. And indeed, one can find studies that claim that dry cat food is not a serious problem, but in such things I am inclined to take the side closest to nature, not economics or other artificial considerations.

To begin with, dry foods for cats contain the wrong kind of protein, too many carbohydrates, and not enough water. Start with water. Domestic cats, like the wild ones, have what can be thought of as a low thirst drive. Cats have evolved to get most of the water they need from their diet of meat, which is made up of about 75 percent water. Dry foods contain only about 10 percent water, and without a lot of added water, the cat is headed for low-level dehydration, which has some very unpleasant long-term effects. Even with water added to the cat's diet, it is likely to get only about half of what it should. (Cats groom themselves so much that they typically use up half their daily intake in that activity.) Terrible things await a chronically dehydrated or not fully hydrated cat. Among them are kidney and bladder problems that will end up being extremely painful and can ultimately be lethal. Indeed, renal failure is one of the more common causes of cat mortality.

Now take the matter of protein. Not all protein is the same. Protein that is found in meat (typically animal muscle as opposed to what are called on labels animal "by-products") contains all of the necessary amino acids required by a cat. Plant protein is biologically less valuable to a cat: not only does it lack certain needed amino acids, but the cat's digestive system (its digestive enzymes) did not evolve to obtain great food value from plant-derived protein. Even the shorter digestive tract of cats militates against food derived from plants. Most dry foods (including those supposedly scientifically designed for cats) neglect the science of zoology, being primarily made up of plants like corn, wheat, and soya. In dry food, even whatever meat or meat by-products that are included have been cooked at enormous length to render them dry, meaning that they too have less biological value to the cat.

While lacking in the proper kind of protein, dry foods typically contain far too many carbohydrates that, among other things, are not eaten by cats in the wild. Too many carbohydrates in a cat's diet promote both obesity (a common problem for many house cats, dogs, and other domestic animals) and diabetes, which is not just debilitating but leads to blindness and as often as not premature death. (There are some provisional studies that suggest that it is not the carbohydrates that cause diabetes in cats, but mainly a too-rapid weight gain from too much cat food altogether.) Many oft-recommended commercial cat foods for obese cats are labeled "light." This of course means they contain *more* carbohydrates.

The ideal answer is not simply to convert to canned cat food (and this can take some time and tactics if the cat is happy with dry food and the artificial meat flavoring with which it has been impregnated). It is important to read the label on the can. Many contain meat by-products as the chief source of protein, and organs such as liver. Indeed, if possible, avoid canned cat food that is made up of "chicken by-products," for example (meaning feathers and feet and so forth), or "chicken by-product meal" or "broth" or "liver." Chicken meal denotes that it came from chicken muscle (which is what you want) but the word "meal" means it has been cooked for a long time at a high temperature and is therefore much less biologically valuable.

Straight muscle, be it from chicken, lamb, or whatever, is what should be the first thing mentioned on the label, meaning that it is the most plentiful ingredient; corn, wheat, and soya should not be included anywhere, and if plant food is included it should be from rice, oats, or barley and not amount to more than 10 percent.

A common apologia for dry cat food, by the way, is that it promotes dental health, being crunchy and therefore scraping away plaque. But dry food is brittle and only shatters without scraping the cat's teeth. Instead, little pieces of it may get caught between the cat's teeth (that evolved to shear meat, not crack hard things) and become sugar and acid. In fact, most cats swallow the kibble bits whole. Cats do not floss, and dry food doesn't either.

An excellent source of information that adds detail to the caveats above can be found on catinfo.org, where Lisa Pierson lays out the basics of cat nutrition and provides helpful tips on how to help a fussy cat make the transition from dry to wet food, as well as listing some of the most appropriately configured commercial cat foods, not to mention recipes for making cat food at home. In addition, Elizabeth Hodgkins's book on cat nutrition, listed in the Further Reading section, is excellent.

A further word of caution: bringing this matter up to dyed-in-the-wool cat owners can in some cases bring forth what animal behaviorists call distance-increasing signals. In other words, many people simply don't want to believe any of this. The pet food industry will aver that its products have been created with rigorous attention to the cat's nutritional needs. It will also say that eating nothing but wet food is bad for a cat, and cite recent findings that show cats on dry food do not end up with diabetes any more than cats on wet food.

Indeed, there is some evidence that the domestic cat's gut is slightly longer than that of its wild progenitor, the African wild cat, potentially an adaptation to nonmeat food. This is a pretty quick evolutionary change in anatomy, given the fact that dry food for cats is less than a century or so old.

APPENDIX C
Feline Health Problems by Breed

reeding animals like cats and dogs for specific traits, particularly matters of mere appearance, can bring about unintended results including congenital health problems, and has done so frequently. The breeding of dogs for appearance -type traits has gone on longer and more intensely than such breeding among cats, and the list of dog breeds and their associated health problems is a long one. But some breeds of domestic cat have, unfortunately, been found with tendencies to have certain afflictions; they are listed here. A rule of thumb is that the older the breed, the greater likelihood of accumulating health problems. This of course does not mean that every member of a breed will experience congenital health problems. Instead, it means that the particular breed has a certain proneness to them.

Responsible cat breeders are well aware of these problems and make efforts in their breeding programs (typically by means of outbreeding) to lessen them. Local veterinarians can often supply useful insights into these matters and should be consulted where possible. Responsible breeders will have no difficulty answering questions about their breeding programs and the problems of congenital ailments.

Abyssinian
Baldness from compulsive
pulling hair out
Gingivitis

American Curl
Ear infections

Balinese (modern wedge-type)
Heart disease
Upper-respiratory infections

Bengal
Loose kneecap
Oversensitivity to anesthetics,
vaccines, pesticides

Bombay (contemporary-type only)
Cleft palate
Skull and tooth malformations

British Shorthair
Heart disease
Hemophilia B
Loose kneecap

Burmese
Pulling hair out
Skull and jaw malformations
Vestibular disease

Chantilly/Tiffany
Stress when left alone

Chartreux
Loose kneecap

Cornish Rex
Heart disease
Thyroid deficiencies

Devon Rex
Heart disease
Hip dysplasia
Loose kneecap
Spasticity

Egyptian Mau
Oversensitivity to anesthetics,
vaccines, pesticides

Exotic Shorthair
Excessive tear flow

Sinus problems

Havana
Respiratory infections

Himalayan
Excessive tear flow (modern
breeds only)

Oversensitivity of the senses

Pulling out hair

Sinus problems (modern breeds
only)

Korat
Respiratory infections

Oversensitivity to anesthetics,
vaccines, pesticides

Maine Coon
Hip dysplasia

Manx
Central nervous system diseases

Corneal dystrophy

Spina bifida

Norwegian Forest
Hip dysplasia

Oriental Shorthair
Heart disease

Oversensitivity to anesthetics,
vaccines, pesticides

Respiratory infections

Persian
Excessive tear flow

Heart disease

Inward-folded eyelids

Retinal degeneration

Skin sensitivities

Stenosis (narrowing) of tear
ducts

Upper, lower teeth don't meet
(Peke-faced type only)

Scottish Fold
Bone degeneration

Excessive tear flow

Oversensitivity to anesthetics,
vaccines, pesticides

Sinus problems

Siamese
Central nervous system diseases

Enlargement of ribs and ends of
long bones

Heart disease

Pulling out hair

Respiratory infections

Undeveloped upper eyelid

Vestibular disease

Somali
> Gingivitis

Sphynx
> Easy loss of body heat
> Heart disease
> Oversensitivity to anesthetics,
>   vaccines, pesticides

Tonkinese
> Oversensitivity to anesthetics,
>   vaccines, pesticides
> Respiratory infections

Turkish Angora
> Deafness
> Loose kneecap

White Domestic Shorthair/Longhair
> Deafness in cats with blue eyes
> Skin cancer

Acknowledgments

Embarking on the adventure that is implicit in writing a book, one has to begin climbing up on the shoulders of others who have plied the same territory, and the people whose names and works appear next, in the Further Reading section, are duly and profoundly thanked for their insights and information (happily swiped). I am indebted also to the several Sallys and other friends whose cat tales have enlivened this book. My wife Susanne is at least a silent partner in all these enterprises and, in this one, performed important research—impelled by hearing that the feral cats around here were obligate carnivores. This led to the startling (to me) analysis of cat nutrition that comprises Appendix B: Cat Food Alert.

Once a book is written, it becomes even more of a joint venture, beginning (if the author is lucky) with comments from someone with a lifetime of expertise such as Michael W. Fox. The careful and creative attention of a dogged editor and then champion (in this case Elisabeth Dyssegaard, executive editor of Smithsonian Books) is essential, as are the efforts of a really ferociously dogged copy editor (Suzanne Fass), the calm assistant copy chief (Amy Vreeland), a lively book designer with a sense of humor (Chris Welch), and many others involved in seeing the book into print. I am, in all of this, greatly blessed. And now it is all up to my old friend, Bruce Nichols, publisher at Collins Books.

Further Reading

Authors like cats because they are such quiet, lovable, wise creatures and cats like authors for the same reasons.

—ROBERTSON DAVIES

Alderton, David. *Cats.* 2nd ed. New York: Dorling Kindersley, Smithsonian Handbooks, 2003.

Barcott, Bruce. "Kill the Cat that Kills the Bird?" *The New York Times Magazine*, December 2, 2007.

Beadle, Muriel. *The Cat: History, Biology, and Behavior.* New York: Simon and Schuster, 1977.

Beaver, Bonnie V. *Feline Behavior: A Guide for Veterinarians.* St. Louis: W. B. Saunders Company, 2003.

Becker, Marty. *Do Cats Always Land on Their Feet?* Deerfield Beach, FL: Health Communications, Inc., 2006.

Bekoff, Marc and John A. Byers, eds. *Animal Play.* Cambridge and New York: Cambridge University Press, 1998.

Budiansky, Stephen. *The Character of Cats.* New York: Viking, 2002.

Caras, Roger. *A Cat Is Watching.* New York: Simon and Schuster, 1989.

Clutton-Brock, Juliet. *A Natural History of Domesticated Animals.* 2nd ed. Cambridge and New York: Cambridge University Press, 1999.

Colbert, Edwin H. *Evolution of the Vertebrates*. 3rd ed. New York: John Wiley & Sons, 1980.

Eliot, T. S. *Old Possum's Book of Practical Cats*. New York: Harcourt Brace and Co., 1939.

Estes, Richard D. *The Safari Companion*. White River Junction, Vermont: Chelsea Green Publishing Company, 1999.

Fagen, Robert. *Animal Play Behavior*. New York: Oxford University Press, 1981.

Fogle, Bruce. *The Cat's Mind*. New York: Macmillan Publishing, 1992.

Fox, Michael W. *Understanding Your Cat*. Revised edition. New York: St. Martin's Press, 1991.

————. *Cat Body, Cat Mind*. Guilford, CT: The Lyons Press, 2007.

Hausman, Gerald and Loretta. *The Mythology of Cats*. New York: St. Martin's Press, 1998.

Hodgkins, Elizabeth M. *Your Cat: Simple New Secrets to a Longer, Stronger Life*. New York: St. Martin's Press, 2007.

Houpt, Katherine A. *Domestic Animal Behavior*. 4th ed. Ames, Iowa: Blackwell Publishing, 2005.

Hubbell, Sue. *Shrinking the Cat*. Boston: Houghton Mifflin Company, 2001.

Kitchener, Andrew. *The Natural History of Wild Cats*. Ithaca, New York: Comstock Publishing Associates, 1991.

Kobalenko, Jerry. *Forest Cats of North America*. Willowdale, Ontario: Firefly Books, 1997.

Kreuz, Tamara. *The Stray Cat Handbook*. New York: Howell Book House, 1999.

Kurtén, Björn. *Before the Indians*. New York: Columbia University Press, 1988.

Marks, Anne. *The Cat in History, Legend, and Art*. London: Elliot Stock, 1909.

Marquis, Don. *The Annotated Archy and Mehitabel*. Edited by Michael Sims. New York: Penguin, 2006.

Morris, Desmond. *Cat Watching*. New York: Crown Publishers, 1986.

Quammen, David. *Monster of God*. New York: W.W. Norton, 2003.

Simon, John M. with Stephanie Pedersen. *What Your Cat Is Trying to Tell You*. New York: St. Martin's Press, 1998.

Turner, Alan. *The Big Cats and Their Fossil Relatives*. New York: Columbia University Press, 1997.

Turner, Dennis C. and Patrick Bateson, eds. *The Domestic Cat: The Biology of Its Behavior*. Cambridge and New York: Cambridge University Press, 2000.

Wallin, Pamela. *The Comfort of Cats*. Amherst, New York: Prometheus Books, 2003.

Zoran, Debra L. "The Carnivore Connection in Cats." *Journal of the American Veterinary Medical Association* 221, no. 11 (2002): 1559–67.

Index

Page numbers in *italics* refer to illustrations.